Cutler and Huntsberry have ~~changed thousands of people's lives~~ *– including mine – through their workshops. Finally, they have made their wisdom available to everyone in their new book ... an inspiration to read, and a joy to live.*

~ Laura Fraser
Author of *An Italian Affair*

A truly remarkable transference of insights from improvisational dance to the human dance in which we all are engaged. An inspiring handbook for living wherever you may be on life's path.

~ L. Freeman Dhority, Ph.D.
Director, Project Dialogue
Author of *Joyful Fluency*

My experience in forty years of international diplomatic service is that fear lies at the bottom of most human conflict, and Americans are more fear-driven than any people I've known. As **Creative Listening** *confirms, the only remedy I have found for fear and the conflict it incites rests in the power of listening, with its ability to create human intimacy. If you're concerned with human conflict on any level, read this book.*

~ Robert Luneburg
U.S. Diplomat, retired
Development & Disaster Response

Every human knows the power of fear and how it limits our freedom. This book brilliantly points the way toward true empowerment, using stories of listening with our whole being, not just our ears. For me, the most memorable advice was what to do when inspiration fails: "repeat, borrow, or be still." I can't wait to share this with my clients!

~ Elizabeth K. Olson
President, Preferred Futures, Inc.

The threshold quotes are a treasure trove; and the reliable companion pieces of exposition and experiences are thoughtful, personal, almost addictive.

~ Heather Howard
Corporate Attorney

A wonderful perspective on fear and its relationship to living freely. Ran and Chery's stories helped me become conscious of how a life of freedom is a life of creative improvisation.

~ Roger J. Henderson
Leadership, Engineering, &
Communications Coach
Aerospace Industry

What a joy to sit in the unknown and just listen ... intently; to discover that strength is a function of flexibility, and that confidence comes from calming the momentum. Wise counsel from two who have spent their lifetimes sharing their passions with those of us lucky enough to listen and embrace the dance!

~ Ann Kram
Visual Arts Instructor & Artist

Just when we've been convinced that the rational mind waltzes us into the realm of authoritative constitution, we find Cutler and Huntsberry's research on the slippery dimensions of the improvisational process reawakening our desire to dance our way back to the authentic moment of our humble origins – playing awake! Listening fearlessly!

~ Pedro Alejandro
Chair, Department of Dance,
Wesleyan University

This book is a gift. I got completely lost in the wonderful stories and wisdom of the text.

> **~ Barry Grosskopf, M.D.**
> Psychiatrist
> Author of *Healing the Generations:*
> *How Understanding Your Family*
> *Legacy Can Transform Your Life*

Creative Listening *brings into reach and reason precepts and skills that create connections to all that surrounds us. The reader-friendly format offers compelling justification to be unafraid in our daily lives and genuinely receptive to our own power and possibilities.*

> **~ Mary Zinn**
> President, Zinn Mediation Associates

Chery and Ran invite us to trust the intuitive wisdom of our collective consciousness, and unlock again the energy, creativity, brilliance – and joy – that were always there.

> **~ Kaye M. Shackford**
> Author of *Charting a Wiser Course:*
> *How Aviation Can Address*
> *the Human Side of Change*

Creative Listening

Also by Randall Huntsberry:

Listening Out Loud: The Leadership Paradox (2001)

Creative Listening

Overcoming Fear in Life & Work

Cheryl Varian Cutler & Randall Huntsberry

iUniverse, Inc.
New York   Lincoln   Shanghai

Creative Listening
Overcoming Fear in Life & Work

iUniverse books may be ordered through booksellers or by contacting:

iUniverse
2021 Pine Lake Road, Suite 100
Lincoln, NE 68512
www.iuniverse.com
1-800-Authors (1-800-288-4677)

Because of the dynamic nature of the Internet, any Web addresses or links contained in this book may have changed since publication and may no longer be valid.

The views expressed in this work are the authors' and do not necessarily reflect the views of the publisher, and the publisher hereby disclaims any responsibility for them.

Front Cover photo:
Myrtle, Tarkine Wilderness
by Robert John Blakers

Back Cover photos:
by Diane Smyth

ISBN: 978-0-595-47024-2 (pbk)
ISBN: 978-0-595-91308-4 (ebk)

Printed in the United States of America

for our parents,

whose listening spoke louder than words

Contents

ACKNOWLEDGMENTS

We extend our gratitude to so many for their contributions to our work over the years. First, our former students at Wesleyan University and the participants of our workshops, who joined us at the most vital level, exploring ideas through movement improvisation, and sharing invaluable insights into the material that has become this book.

Along with these contributors, we wish to honor colleagues from our early explorations into improvisation as a performing art, not the least of whom are the other original members of *Sonomama Improvisational Dance Theater*: Joan Burbick, Charles Kreiner, Susan Lourie, Willa Needler, and David Rynick. They were pioneers with us in this uncharted territory, and memories of those early years continue to provide inspiration for our work today. A debt of gratitude is due as well to dance colleagues working in other forms of improvisation, whose parallel explorations enriched our own: Susan Leigh Foster, George Russell, Cynthia Novack, and Richard Bull.

We are deeply indebted to Chuck Gregory for his help in preparing this manuscript and its cover for publication. Besides considerable editorial skills, he brought equanimity, patience, and acuity to his repeated readings of the text.

We also wish to thank our many friends and colleagues who generously read and tirelessly edited prior drafts: Karen Aubrey, Alan Barber, Debbie Bower, Anita Bondi, Angelina Citron, Marleen Dean, Robin Dellabough, Judy Dworin, Regina Giannini, Martha Lask, Myron and Penina Glazer, Heather Howard, Mark Knowles, Deenah Loeb, Wendy Lustbader, Karyn Mandan, Elizabeth Olson, Andrea Shaw Reed, Elizabeth Rees, Sally Robinson, Catherine Royce, Arielle Shanok, Stan Stewart Sawyer, Gerrit Stover (the first to encourage us to write this book), Erik Sween, Suzanna

Tamminen, Kaethe Weingarten, and Jeremy Zwelling. Above all, we are grateful to those friends who allowed us to include their very special life stories here.

Finally, our loving appreciation goes out to our families. It was at their kitchen tables that our partnership, *Listening Unlimited*, was born. With their creative, critical, professional, organizational, and financial support, we were able to set this dream in motion. Today, their rigorous honesty and wisdom continue to guide and sustain us. Our very special thanks go to Kristen and Tom Bissinger, Enid Ellison Cutler, Joy and Thor Cutler, Steve Huntsberry and Kathy Dean, Marsha and Bruce Kerr, Joan Huntsberry, Shannon and David Hawley, Claire Huntsberry, and David B. Hawley.

Creative Listening

INTRODUCTION

What does it take to overcome fear? In a word, *listening*.

In the face of fear – from low-level anxiety to full-blown panic – listening can unfold answers for what to do or say. Though the most simple and humble of acts, listening is a source not only of everyday solutions, but of unlimited discovery and creativity.

With dedicated practice and experience, confidence grows in the power of listening. And as confidence grows, fear diminishes, step by step.

Learning to quiet fear and to listen three-dimensionally – to one's own inner voice, to others, and to the environment – is a practice we call *creative listening*.

Universal in nature and applicable in any field of endeavor, creative listening is an essential skill for lawyers, teachers, ministers, artists, athletes, corporate executives, spouses, parents, anyone who has to think on his or her feet – and communicate. Tested in a wide variety of contexts, creative listening has proven to be nothing less than *the essential discipline of creativity itself*.

We stumbled upon this discovery in performing with a dance improvisation company, *Sonomama[1] Improvisation Dance Theater*. Over the years, learning to apply creative listening, not only to the stage but to virtually every pursuit in our lives, *became* our lives – and eventually, the inspiration for this book.

---

1   '*Sonomama*' is Japanese for 'Just as it is.'

IMPROVISATION

Always do what you are afraid to do.

~ Ralph Waldo Emerson

To improvise is to act spontaneously, without previous preparation, to devise, compose, or perform something on the spur of the moment.

Some people resort to improvisation as an approach to solving problems when no obvious answer is available. Others use it as a method for generating new, creative material. In either case, improvisation serves an auxiliary function: it is a means to an end, not an end in itself.

In our work with *Sonomama*, however, we viewed improvisation differently. As an improvisational performing company, we created our dances at the moment of their performance. The process of improvisation *was* our product; the means *was* our end.

In time, we moved beyond even this idea. We came to regard improvisation not only as a resource for creative ideas, or even an artistic product, but as the essence of creativity. We realized that in viewing an improvisational performance, an audience was actually watching the very process of creative thought.

Sharing how an understanding of this process can enrich all aspects of life has turned out to be, in some fundamental sense, central to the life-paths we were each impelled to take. And this is the subject of our story.

BEGINNINGS

In my beginning is my end.

~ T. S. Eliot

The morning was unseasonably warm, almost balmy. We pulled off at a small roadside restaurant, *Me and McGee's* (formerly known as *Bobby's*), a favorite hangout for locals and a get-away place for faculty and students with wheels.

Over a reunion breakfast, we laughed and talked. "The single most vital thing I've learned in my educational career," Chery reminisced, "is what we discovered in *Sonomama* – the practice of listening."

"Really?" Ran looked surprised. "That's just what I would say. Teaching, family counseling, corporate coaching, poetry, you name it – all of it has been improvisation and the practice of listening."

We first met in 1970 as freshmen faculty at Wesleyan University. Our paths had since diverged, and for more than twenty-five years, we had lost contact. But this casual conversation was about to launch a whole new endeavor for us both. It would open the way to our co-leading workshops from coast to coast, and eventually to co-authoring this book.

Just how this all came about we could never have predicted even in our most creative flights of imagination.

THE DISCIPLINE OF CREATIVITY

The essential often appears
at the end of a long conversation.
The great truths are spoken
on the doorstep.

~ E. M. Cioran

When we co-founded *Sonomama* in the early '70s, Chery was a dance professor and Ran a professor in comparative religions at Wesleyan.

Our collaboration lasted a brief five years before Ran left and headed west. Years later in a moment of reflection, Chery realized how deeply affected her career had been by the ideas Ran brought to their early explorations.

On an impulse, she tracked Ran down with a phone call to the other side of the country. As if no time had elapsed, our conversation picked up right where we had left off decades before.

That early morning at *McGee's*, we realized that though our lives had taken very different directions, we had come to virtually identical conclusions:

- We wanted to live as creatively as we had danced.

- Listening was the key to creativity in life as well as in improvisation.

- Fear was what got in the way of listening.

- Strategies we had formulated to face fear, handle its negative effects, and free our creativity in dance improvisation applied as aptly to our everyday lives as they did to the performance stage.

After several casual but unusually exciting conversations over a period of a year and a half, we decided to share what we had learned through a series of workshops we called *Creative Listening: Improvisation as Life Practice*.

Movement as Medium

*Mr. Duffy lived a short distance
from his body.*

~ James Joyce

From our very earliest collaborations, movement improvisation was the laboratory for our experiments in creativity. It remains today our basic medium for teaching creativity and communicating concepts.

Movement is ideal for exploring creativity, in large part because of its gift for concretizing the abstract. Action *realizes* thought. It brings both the conscious and the subliminal into view, rendering invisible thoughts, feelings, and relationships visible.

Because of its unique capabilities for exemplifying creativity, we will employ movement improvisation throughout this text as illustrative example. However, movement exercises *per se* will not be our main focus. The spectrum of our interest is far broader: creativity itself.

Initially, movement may appear an unlikely medium of exploration and discourse, especially for adults. A mature person all too often connotes a sedentary one. But we have found movement surprisingly effective in working with an adult population.

Assumptions and habits are less embedded in an unfrequented venue, and the very unfamiliarity of movement seems to encourage creativity. Further, using their bodies helps adults 'get out of their heads,' freeing up their ability to see things differently.

At first, leaving the safety of language and stepping out into the medium of movement may seem risky to some workshop participants. But often this simple act of courage is just what induces the openness and receptivity necessary for creative change.

COLLABORATIVE WRITING

The world is divided into people
who think they are right.

~ Anonymous

If action is essential to the creative experiment, reflection is equally so. Within our workshops, as well as in our life-experience with improvisation, reflection has always companioned action. So it is not surprising that, after several years of workshop development and teaching, we have now entered a new stage in our collaboration, the writing of this book.

We have taken up this challenge for two reasons: a lifelong commitment to *creativity* and an equally keen interest in *communication*.

Our choice to focus on communication stems from a shared conviction in the power of listening to heal fear-based conflict and promote cooperation. Ironically, nowhere has this conviction been more truly tested for us than in our collaborative efforts with one another.

When we co-founded *Sonomama*, we had no idea how different the two of us really were. Our commitment to the exploration of movement and creativity drew us together. But beyond this point of commonality, we soon proved poles apart in how we viewed the world – in fact, how we saw the very nature of R/reality itself.

Chery has a deeply committed faith and believes that the spiritual realm is the eternal and 'Real.' Ran is agnostic by 'faith' and believes that the 'truth' one individual negotiates with another in ordinary conversation is as 'real' as it gets.

What we have gained from our years of association is a certainty that if individuals as different as the two of us can sustain so rich a collaboration, then there is more potential for cooperation among disparate mentalities than a reasonable person might imagine.

Our second reason for undertaking this book centers on creativity and our belief that, from our combined years of work in artistic, corporate, therapeutic, religious, and academic environments, we have learned something about living creatively. Specifically, about living creatively in the face of fear.

We are convinced that the keystone of creativity is listening, because listening generates the discovery of new ideas. But what is more, we have found that inherent in any idea is its own best expression. If we will only *listen* or pay attention to an idea *without fear*, precise expressions of that idea, ones best suited to its given context, will naturally surface.

What holds true in listening to and communicating ideas also holds true in communicating with people. By listening to others openly and without fear, we all find ourselves capable of clearer self-expression, greater creativity, and deeper understanding.

MAGIC BULLETS

Nothing that is worth knowing
can be taught.

~ Oscar Wilde

In an age when many seem desperate to acquire a competitive edge, we focus here on exploring our 'creative edge.' Rather than a means of gaining power over others, *creative listening* is a way to reach and fully realize our own individual potential.

At the same time, we want to emphasize that our goal is not to provide readers with self-help tricks or magic bullets. It is instead to explore the broader practice and power of listening, which each person may apply as he or she chooses.

We are all hungry for answers, but it would be misleading to imagine that formulaic solutions can be found to questions as deep as how to access the source of creativity or heal human conflict. Even though we know this, facile answers can often seem seductive, and we may be tempted to grasp at these will-o-the-wisps, thinking now we have really *got* something.

Chery & Ran: In a popular 19th century grammar, Swinton's Fourth Reader[2], there is a story told of the 'key flower,' where a shepherd, tending his sheep in the mountains, comes upon a strange, unassuming flower. He stoops to pick it, and suddenly an open door appears, one he has never seen before, set in the mountainside.

Through the door, he enters a tunnel into an underground chamber. To his amazement, he finds the chamber heaped with jewels and gold and guarded by an old dwarf.

---

2   William Swinton, *Swinton's Fourth Reader*, New York: American Book Co., 1883.

The dwarf welcomes him to as much of the treasure as he can carry, but admonishes firmly, "Don't forget the best." Placing the flower on a nearby table, the shepherd proceeds to fill his pockets. As he turns to leave, he hears again, "Don't forget the best!"

Upon passing through the little door into the open air, the shepherd feels his pockets grow light. The door has vanished, and his treasure has turned to dry leaves and pebbles. Then he recalls the forgotten flower, left behind.

Like the key flower, the mental state of *listening without fear*, what we call *the improvisational mind*, does not look like much. In fact, it is empty of content. But this state of mind is the key; it is receptivity itself.

We have no store of ready-made answers to suggest, just a state of mind and practice, practice, practice. For us, there are no quick fixes. Like the dwarf, who points to the key flower as the real treasure, we would rather help others to come up with their own answers, for their own lives, in their own ways.

Ways to Read this Book

Traveler, there is no path.
Paths are made by walking.

~ Antonio Machado

The pace of modern life is so rapid, so filled with activities and distractions, that the idea of yet another book added to the pile of those already unread seems almost too much. Where will we find the time?

For this reason, we have purposely designed this text to give readers a choice: to read the book from cover to cover following a loosely linear progression of ideas, or to approach it non-linearly, entering from myriad angles like the spokes of a wheel converging on its hub.

The quickest of these non-linear approaches is to open at random and read a quote from one of the many authors we cite. Another is to read and ponder just one paragraph – any paragraph in the non-italicized text. A third is to turn to a single italicized section for a short story. And a fourth alternative is to select one chapter from anywhere in the book and read that chapter as a discrete entity.

The text is divided into three parts. *Part I* presents our general thesis and basic concepts. *Part II* expands these ideas and their applications in multiple directions. And *Part III* explores the practice of creative listening in three specific social contexts.

Understanding ideas, indeed living life itself, has both linear and non-linear aspects. We invite you to enter into this discourse in whatever way best suits you. One request only: that you not simply *read* the ideas, but take time to *listen* to them, and mark their reverberations, as you go.

PART ONE

FEAR

Some things'll scare you so bad,
you'll hurt yourself.

~ Boots Cooper, age 8,

after a close encounter

with a chicken snake

How many of us have had to face an audience and perform without a script, making it up as we went along? Performing improvisationally is not most people's idea of fun!

But we are all called upon, sooner or later, both to think creatively and to perform publicly. At the very least, the small and large crises of daily life compel us to think on our feet.

By using movement improvisation as a means, this book explores the central discipline of creativity: listening. And it confronts the main obstruction to creativity: fear.

Creativity is essentially the practice of listening without fear. Within this practice lie immediate answers to any situation where creative imagination or problem solving is required.

Over thirty years ago, through our explorations with *Sonomama Improvisation Dance Theater*, we unexpectedly happened upon some fundamental answers to the question of how to overcome fear. Precursors of these discoveries, however, hearken all the way back to some of our earliest memories.

Ran: By the time I was in the second grade, my family had moved thirteen times, and each new playground was terrifying. I was deathly afraid of the other boys and was uncertain of my place in the pecking order. There were daily fistfights.

13

Years later, my mother recollected, "Not a week went by that I wasn't called into the principal's office!"

Yet even more threatening than the schoolyard were my father's frequent absences from home on business trips. From early on, I was left surrogate 'head-of-household' and my mother's 'caretaker.'

Doubtless, to the adults, 'caretaker' was meant as little more than a figure of speech, but to me, it signaled a solemn responsibility. Coupled with my playground anxieties, fearful feelings of inadequacy over this charge soon resulted in increasingly serious acts of rebellion.

When I was twelve or so, my best friend and I were almost caught stealing two .38 caliber pistols from a local hardware store. We escaped, running frantically through backstreets and alleys all the way home.

When I entered the kitchen, my mother met me with news of another friend apprehended that morning for stealing a car. Having barely caught my breath from my own near disaster, I heard her say, "I am so relieved I don't have to worry about you doing anything like that!"

All of a sudden, it hit me. My violence and vandalism, if discovered, would devastate my mother. My reaction to an overwhelming sense of responsibility for her had ironically transformed into a serious threat to her well-being.

I realized then that the best protection I could afford her was to change my own behavior. From that point on, I never stole again or got into another fight.

The gentle influence of empathy has extraordinary power. At that moment in my life, it changed everything for me – at least for the time being.

Years later as a workaholic graduate student in Japan, I confronted even more intimidating circumstances than those I had faced as a child. I went suddenly blind in one eye, a frightening event in any case, but a daunting impairment for a research scholar who read most of his waking hours.

At first, I ignored – or better, denied – what had happened to me. Japanese doctors diagnosed the blindness as a symptom of multiple sclerosis. Though the steroids they put me on did not restore my sight, they gave me superhuman energy and sustained my denial for a while longer.

Then one day, I collapsed from utter exhaustion. The doctors immediately took me off the steroids, and within three months, my sight miraculously returned. Off the hook, I dove back into my studies.

Soon after returning to the States, my legs went numb. Harvard doctors asserted that if I did not bounce back within three months, as I had in Japan, I could probably look forward to a gradual decline into total paralysis. I would become a mind trapped inside a lifeless body, unable to move or communicate – my worst nightmare.

I resolved to do something radically different. In response to the 'nervous breakdown' MS represented, I determined to give up trying to 'make it' according to the norms of university life.

I am my consciousness, I reasoned, and to the degree my mind is overwrought, I am overwrought; to the degree it is unconscious, I am unconscious. So what I have to do is to 'change my mind.' From this moment of realization, my focus shifted from entrapment to freedom and from compulsivity to creativity.

In order to live the most creative, effective, and resourceful life, Ran realized he had to quiet fear and listen to his own inner voice. Later, he found that Chery in her own way had come to a similar conclusion.

Chery: *The nightmare always began the same way – outside a dance studio just as class is to commence or backstage as the curtain is about to rise. All of a sudden, I am urgently informed that I am expected to teach the class or enter a dance performance already begun.*

I have no idea what the class plan is. And I have never even seen the dance, let alone been to a rehearsal. Panic-stricken, I protest. But my pleas fall on deaf ears. I have to step up, I am told; there is no one else to take my place.

I find myself pushed out before a class of expectant students or a sea of upturned faces in a darkened theater. I stare at them all in silent dismay. One by one, the moments tick by. Gradually, the interest of disappointed students or a disgruntled audience wanes. My opportunity ebbs away.

Over the years, I have awakened from this nightmare in a sweat more times than I can remember. One day I recounted the dream to a friend.

"What's so scary about that?" he asked.

I tried to explain. "Well, life hands us a few prime moments to do what we care most about doing, give what we care most about giving. If we miss them," I agonized, "they are surely lost forever."

"So, what is it you want to give?" he wanted to know.

That was hard to say. "I don't know. My best? Whatever of value I've figured out about life? Whatever I have worth sharing?"

"Yourself, it sounds like," he said.

"OK … yes," I said hesitatingly, "myself – sort of."

"Well then, just stand there and be yourself," he said.

"Oh my glory, that wouldn't do. No way would I be adequate!" I was horrified. "But if I were given enough time," I added hopefully, "maybe I could prepare something that was."

In the days that followed, this conversation replayed over and over in my mind. The nature of the fear that terrorized my dreams had been revealed, and I could not forget it.

There is no running away from reoccurring nightmares. They return unbidden. I would have to confront them head on, to do in my waking hours what I feared most to do in my dreams: face the world without a script … and be good enough. But how was I ever to do that?

Within weeks, Ran approached me with a wild idea he had had of forming an improvisational performance group. I could only laugh – my nightmare realized!

FIRST STEPS

The poem asks only
that the poet get out of the way.

~ Donald Hall

Chery: *I lay on my back with my arms and legs sticking straight up in the air. I wiggled my toes. A dead bug, that was what it felt like. A dead bug. How creative was that?*

What was I doing? September would be here any moment. The students would be descending on campus in swarms. Rehearsals for the faculty dance concert would be booked in no time, and what would I have to show? Zilch. I rolled up to standing.

I began to move around in the vast, empty theater. My phrases were smooth and lovely, the sort of conservative, dancerly-type movement I had seen and done a thousand times before. I was sick to death of it. I dropped back down on my back; hands and feet went up again.

This was pitiful. No one would ever want to watch this. Then I thought, "But face it – it's better than what you usually do! It's actually new."

At that moment, both literally and figuratively, I had dropped as low as I could go. What was left to fear? Being a bug on its back, like the nightmare image in Kafka's Metamorphosis, *was more appealing to me than the stale, rote movement I had been generating for what seemed like forever.*

Whatever I did or did not do now, I was not going back to that. "I'll lie here all August, if I have to," I told myself. I was done trying to 'make something up.' I would simply pay attention to whatever was actually happening – here and now – and that was it.

By the end of that two-hour session, I found myself on my feet. I had not meant to stand. I had just arrived somehow. For the first time in ages, the movement I was doing was new!

Many times since, when the beginning of some endeavor has seemed unpromising, Chery has gratefully recalled this incident and the Persian proverb, "All newborns are ugly."

CONFRONTING FEAR

… the best way out is always through.

~ Robert Frost

When *Sonomama* first began regular exploratory practice sessions, the freedom and creativity we experienced were intoxicating. All sorts of new material emerged. But our euphoria was short lived.

Within less than a year, we noticed our work had become repetitious, predictable. This was not at all the creative adventure that we had originally experienced and had envisioned would continue indefinitely.

We tried everything we could think of to restore our original excitement, but to no avail. The innocence of what Zen Buddhists call the 'beginner's mind' was gone. Now we would have to dig deeper. We had discovered the source of creative thought – listening. Now we would have to identify and confront whatever stood in its way.

Eventually, we realized we were resorting to familiar movement patterns and were doing so in a consistent way, falling back on these patterns at the moment we either became confused over the direction of the improvisation or lost confidence in the dance altogether.

At these moments, we panicked. We stopped listening to what was actually happening in the here and now, and clutched onto old patterns we hoped might save us. Instead, they sunk us like a stone.

Initially, we tried to deny there was a problem. Then as our improvisations became increasingly stale and boring, we tried to deny that fear had anything to do with it. It was merely a matter of will, we said. Simply avoid habitual patterns and do something else. When this 'just say no' approach failed, we grew more and more frustrated.

It was clear that fear had to be uncovered and handled, one way or another, before we would be able to listen to and hear anything else. The question was how.

Finally, it occurred to us to apply what we had learned from the practice of the Japanese martial art, *Aikido*. In *Aikido*, instead of trying to block an attack, the martial artist side-steps the blow, flows with the direction of the thrust, and then uses the energy of the attack to throw or pin the attacker.

Adopting this approach, we reversed our confrontational strategy. Instead of trying to block our fear-based responses, we identified these patterns explicitly and made them the starting point of our improvisations. Just as the martial artist uses the energy of his or her assailant to nullify and reverse an attack, we transformed our fears into a creative resource.

KOANS

If you cannot get rid of the family skeleton,
you may as well make it dance.

~ George Bernard Shaw

By identifying the repetitive, fear-based patterns in each dancer's movement vocabulary, patterns by now clearly predictable, we highlighted the most common escape route each member of *Sonomama* adopted in response to fear. We then froze that particular movement pattern into a single, set posture. These physical postures we called our 'koans.'

We borrowed the notion of koans from Zen Buddhism. In this tradition, koans are stories or sayings, given to students by their Masters as questions meant to foster and test the students' degree of 'awakening,' or 'enlightenment.'

A koan such as "What is the sound of one hand clapping?" cannot be successfully answered through logic or reason. Only an intuitive, or even counterintuitive, understanding will do. As a result, students typically spend years presenting possible answers to the Master before arriving at an acceptable response.

In *Sonomama*, we viewed our koans, our set postures, as questions meant to test and foster our ability to listen without fear. These physical shapes became our starting points for improvisation after improvisation. And whenever our koans occurred spontaneously in a dance, instead of fighting them, we observed the characteristics of these shapes with curiosity and let them serve as material for further creative exploration.

Koans enabled us to observe exactly when and how fear blocked our creativity. The habitual movement patterns or positions we escaped to in the face of fear, like flares, signaled that we had shut down. And these shutdowns of our attention were what was producing stale, lifeless dances.

Not everyone's fear took the same form, and this fact particularly intrigued us. Our fears did not have a universal shape or content. For example, one person's koan in the company was a low, rounded, crouched position, while another's was tall, narrow, and rigidly upright. Each koan was unique to the individual.

Strangely enough, a dancer, when first confronted with what the group had identified as his or her koan, often had no recognition of the posture. In fact, he or she would emphatically deny that this shape was at all familiar. For a while, this response – and most of us had it – puzzled us.

We eventually realized that when we became fearful, we closed down mentally. We shifted onto automatic pilot. Ceasing to listen, we retreated into a fog of semi-conscious habit. And this fog made our fear, obscured as it was from conscious thought, difficult to corner and confront. Not only the nature of our fears, but their very presence was hidden from us.

Now, through exploring our koans, we were actually able to 'see' our fears, as if in a mirror. In the example cited above of the rigidly upright koan, the dancer's fear of the creative unknown had him retreating into the safety of mechanized movement, of inflexible, mindless, lock-step routine.

As he danced improvisation after improvisation, each begun from this same koan position, we watched him pass though several stages. First, he investigated the symbolic implications of his koan shape. In time, he came to realize that this position represented anything but the safety he had attributed to it. In fact, the rigidity inherent in his shape was actually what most frightened him. Finally, he arrived at a playful relationship with his koan and the fear it symbolized, greatly diffusing its power to block his creativity.

All of us experienced a similar evolution with our koans. Once exposed and repeatedly played out in a succession of dances, our fears and their forms of expression began to transform and eventually even to disappear. But until then, because they represented issues of deep feeling, our koans continued to produce pithy, compelling dances.

COUNTER-KOANS

We become what we behold.

~ Marshall McLuhan

In due course, we developed a second approach for dealing with our fears. We turned them upside down.

Here we identified a fear-based movement pattern and then created a starting position that reversed that pattern's particular nature and qualities. This new position we named the 'counter-koan.' Beginning dances from our counter-koans immediately launched us into fresh, innovative material.

For example, one dancer tended to escape fearful situations by floating upwards and becoming light and lyrical, 'Fred Astaire-ing' her way out of tight spots. The counter-koan we assigned her was to lie belly down.

Almost instantly, she began to move in ways we had never seen her move before. At first, she was sluggish, barely able to lift her limbs. Gradually she evolved like a sea creature emerging from the slime into a powerful, muscular, feline beast on the prowl. With this expanded vocabulary, she opened up a whole new range of expression for herself.

Counter-koans were uncomfortable, but they were also exciting. They immediately presented alternative movement options for each of us that we would not have readily accessed otherwise. They provided a stepping-stone out of our ruts of fear by introducing us to unexplored aspects of our own natures.

LIFE IMPLICATIONS

All things change when we do.

~ Master Kukai

As we soon discovered, all of the movement improvisation structures we developed in *Sonomama*, also had implications for fostering and freeing creativity in our lives outside the studio – what we came to call our 'life practice.'

In the case of koans, our basic approach was to identify fear-driven behavior and, rather than attempting to 'fight or flee' it, to make this enemy an ally. We welcomed it, embraced it. We came to know it inside out, exploring it over and over until, out of boredom if nothing else, we broke through its confines into something new.

Chery: A friend of my family, an accomplished opera singer, married a psychiatrist. He came with several children from a former marriage.

One child in the family, an adolescent boy, began stubbornly to protest attending school. After exhausting every other avenue available, the exasperated parents finally made a decision to allow the boy to have his way – to stay at home and just do nothing.

All day, every day, the boy sat in front of the television, eating. Each day he repeated his same ritual – sit, watch, eat – as all the other children went off to school and on to extra-curricular music lessons, sports practices, and social events. One month passed, then another, but no one attempted to persuade the boy to any other course of action.

At the end of a year, grossly overweight and bored silly, he announced to his parents that he wanted to return to school. From that point on, he gave them no more difficulty in this regard. A bright boy, now keenly self-motivated, he resumed his studies with alacrity and went on to complete his education.

Instead of continuing to fight their son's behavior, his parents had at last decided to let the boy embrace his koan every day. Day after day, he had simply acted out his koan until eventually he succeeded in repeating it to death.

This example of employing a real life koan is an extreme case, a last resort when all else failed. While the extremity to which these parents went is not something we would necessarily recommend, in this particular case it worked.

By contrast, counter-koans represent a reverse tactic to overcoming fear.

Ran: [Sam][1] and [Mary] came in for couples counseling. They told me they were having the usual communication problems. When I asked for an example, Mary told me the following story:

"I knew Sam was a spoiled little rich boy when I married him, but it has been worse than I expected. Sam is useless around the house. More than that, he expects me to clean up after him – do his laundry, cook his meals, and worst of all, gather

---

1   Throughout this text, when the actual name of an individual has been replaced by a pseudonym, the pseudonym will appear in brackets when first introduced.

up his dirty dishes from all over the house. I've had it! I've tried everything to change his behavior, and nothing works."

Sam said, a little defensively, that it was "not as bad as all that," but admitted he had a problem cleaning up after himself. I quickly identified to myself Sam's koan: leave everything to Mary. And Mary's koan: pick up after Sam – and occasionally nag. The unconscious repetition of their koans had gotten them nowhere.

A true koan approach, of course, requires conscious awareness. And we could have developed that awareness and gone the koan route. But in the face of Sam and Mary's longstanding impasse, I decided to take a counter-koans approach.

I urged Mary to consider the old adage, "If you can't lick 'em, join 'em.

"Obviously, Sam really values his dishes being dirty," I said, "and apparently would prefer you left them alone, as he does. So why not do it?"

I proposed the following counter-koan for Mary: "Since having to wash Sam's dirty dishes all the time annoys you, stop washing them. Do something different. Instead, move them into his personal space. If you run out of clean dishes, you can shift to paper plates and cups.

"And, since these dirty dishes, and probably his dirty clothes as well, have come between you, I would suggest that you put them all in the middle of your bed, in a long narrow strip, head-to-foot, and as high as need be. When you are no longer comfortable sleeping with all this mess, move to another bed and leave him with his precious garbage."

By now, Mary was howling with delight and crying, "Yes, Yes!" Sam, who had seemed at first taken aback, was laughing too – though with slightly more reserve.

Mary never had to put anything into their bed. Sam got the message. With such a vivid mental image before him, he found it hard to maintain his old, semi-conscious habits. But whenever he did slip up, Mary had only to give him 'that look,' and they both broke up laughing. Good will and a good counter-koan remedied the problem.

Whenever one person in an interaction changes, by definition the interaction itself changes. Discovering different options for ourselves, and acting on them, of necessity confronts others with new choices.

In Mary and Sam's case, Ran did not pursue what was driving their behavior, but experience led him to assume it was some form of fear. There may be other obstacles to interpersonal communication, but fear seems to be by far the most deeply seated and widespread.

To change fear-based behavior in relationships, the koan model involves exposing and diffusing the fear. The counter-koan model entails turning from fear's hypnotic images, looking in the direction to which we would walk, and *walking*.

SELF-DECEPTION AND THE MASKS OF FEAR

I like to know what the truth is
so I can decide whether
to believe it or not.

~ Queen Elizabeth I

The problem of fear is not just its presence, but also its controlling and self-deceptive nature. Undetected, fear directs thought and blocks creativity in more subtle and ubiquitous guises than most of us imagine.

We may occasionally experience naked fear in ourselves or others; but few of us have the courage to face raw fear head-on, day after day. As a result, we avoid dealing with fear altogether by denying its presence, even while it is in full operation and control.

Or more frequently, we experience fear clothed in one of its more palatable guises or masks. These faces of fear include:

Numbness	Passivity
Boredom	Avoidance
Anger	Irresponsibility
Hyper-Control	Withdrawal
Willfulness	Stonewalling
Manipulation	Hauteur
Bullying	Self-Absorption
Domination	Addictive Behavior
Violence	Impatience
'Judgmentalness'	Irritableness
Self-Righteousness	Laziness
Contempt	Distraction
Hate	Hyper-Activity
Over-Commitment	Inordinate Sleep
Under-Commitment	Dread
Dependency	Despair

As we discovered early on in *Sonomama*, these and many other faces of fear appear routinely in movement improvisations and always leave a signature mark. For example, when dancers panic and try to force an improvisation in a certain direction, it looks and feels like the manipulation it is. The dance goes flat, becomes repetitive, loses continuity or energy or direction, or grows either physically dangerous or tedious and predictable.

The presence of fear in day-to-day life produces similar telltale effects. When danger, conflict, or confusion threatens us, we may openly feel and acknowledge fear and respond with panic or violence. More often, however, our fear resides underground, hidden from conscious thought. It may then surface as a relationship gone flat, a career that has lost its vitality and direction, or, as in Ran's case, a failure of health.

OUTSIDE PERSPECTIVE

Nothing is easier than self-deceit.
For what each man wishes,
that he also believes to be true.

~ Demosthenes

Undoubtedly, it takes courage to confront fears hidden by self-deception. Who really wants to look with complete honesty twenty-four hours a day at what he or she is thinking or doing?

Because self-deception in life and in improvisation is unconscious, overcoming the fear behind it is doubly difficult. An outside perspective can help us take the first step by calling attention to our fear-driven behavior.

External feedback enables us to gain perspective on ourselves and on how we are affecting others. In responding to feedback, the courage of honesty is essential. Fear-driven self-deception, if it blocks our receptivity to feedback, can ultimately stymie our creativity – to say nothing of our ability to maintain relationships.

Along with the courage of honesty, the level of receptivity to feedback also depends on individual self-respect, as well as mutual respect and trust between two individuals or among members in a collaborative group. These qualities – respect, trust, and the courage of honesty – are as critical to creative collaboration as they are to any long-term association, personal or professional.

SELF-RIGHTEOUSNESS

It is the characteristic of human nature
to hate the man you have wronged.

~ Tacitus

Self-righteousness, a common knee-jerk reaction to feedback, is one of the most treacherous masks of fear, one we want to give special attention to here because it epitomizes the height of self-deception. When we are feeling self-righteous, we will listen neither to others nor to our own deeper, self-correcting intuitions. We do not feel the need to listen, because we already 'possess the truth.'

Self-righteousness is synonymous with hate; and as stated above, both are masks of fear. To the degree that we are deceived by this fear in disguise, we feel free to 'act out' our feelings and convictions without regard to those around us. People in positions of privilege and power are especially susceptible to the self-indulgence inherent in this form of abuse.

In our immediate relationships, but also as members of the world community, our mutual welfare and ultimately our survival demand that we confront the fear behind self-righteousness, wherever it appears, and strive for transparent communications with our neighbors.

OWNING OUR FEARS

The root of all disturbance,
if one will go to its source,
is that no one will blame himself.

~ Dorotheus of Gaza

In traditional Middle Eastern societies, scapegoats were beasts symbolically laden with the fearful conflicts and ills of the community and then driven off into the desert. All societies display some variation of scapegoating.

It may be tempting to project our faults and fears onto others and blame them for the frightening conditions we experience. But failing to examine our own part in a conflict, blocks any chance for a real solution. Deflecting our problems onto our neighbors only precipitates an inevitable breakdown in possibilities for dialogue and understanding.

Owning our own fears, on the other hand, and gaining an awareness of the fears of others, identifies the underlying issues and brings them to the surface. This provides us with a far more effective means to initiate creative solutions and truly resolve conflicts.

Listening is the universal open hand. It counteracts bigotry, hatred, ignorance, and misunderstanding. Coming from a position of power rather than weakness, it covers and ultimately opens the fist of fear.

OVERCOMING FEAR

Only when we are no longer afraid
do we begin to live.

~ Dorothy Thompson

Our power is defined by the number of options we have and our ability to perceive them. The more options we see, the greater our power.

By closing down our receptivity, fear obstructs our perception of options and, thereby, disempowers us. It blocks our access to our one unlimited source of supply, the ideas and intuitions of the improvisational mind.

As an ideal state free from fear, the improvisational mind is our true source of power. In this receptive state, we find our resources always fully available. Taking advantage of these resources is what appears to the world as creativity.

Therefore, to tap our full power or creative potential, we must learn progressively how to assume the improvisational mind – to overcome fear and listen.

RESPONDING TO FEAR IN DAILY LIFE

Adversity introduces a man to himself.

~ Anonymous

All human beings, at some time and in some way, encounter fear. Situations arise where we feel vulnerable and yet powerless. Our personal resources – whether intellectual, physical, emotional, financial, political, or social – appear inadequate to meet the challenges we face.

In other situations, fear may arise if things are not unfolding according to plan. Having already 'choreographed the dance' in our minds and anticipated its conclusion, we resist any other outcome. Fearful of an unacceptable result, we attempt to will the conclusion according to our own desires.

Whether we find ourselves driven by feelings of inadequacy or by willful desire, we can be certain fear is at the helm of thought. In such cases, what can we do?

A common misconception is that a fear-driven sense of personal responsibility enhances our ability to be responsible, but our experience in improvisation indicates the reverse. The mental state of listening – *responding* to, rather than being *responsible* for, the answers – better enables us to meet life's challenges.

Letting go of the fear underlying a sense of personal responsibility does not make us negligent or irresponsible. Quite the reverse, it opens us up to our full potential for appropriate action.

Similarly, relinquishing willful desire does not disempower us, but allows us to expand the horizon of our expectations, to embrace possibilities for good beyond what we may have first conceived. As experience in improvisation has proven many times over, listening without fear allows the very best scenario to unfold.

Chery: On the early winter's evening when word came down that Ran had lost his bid for tenure, the hopes of friends who had gathered around him to await the verdict were dashed. Only Ran himself seemed undisturbed.

Ran had been conflicted for some time about continuing in academia. He knew his educational views and practices were at odds with the prevailing system.

Friends had urged him to go for tenure to protect the departmental slot; he could always quit later, they coaxed. Although he had heeded their call, he also sensed that the '60s culture of experimentation was over, and that it was time to move on.

I, on the other hand, was profoundly disheartened by the tenure decision. I felt I was losing an irreplaceable colleague. This would bring to an end our exciting collaborations and the future course of Sonomama *as I had imagined it.*

The next evening, following a church meeting, I shared my grief with a friend. When I was finished, she said gently, "There have been times in my life when I wanted something very deeply. I prayed and prayed for a certain outcome. But even our fondest desires can be misguided.

"In one such instance," she continued, "things did not go as I had hoped they might. And I was heartbroken.

"But when we have done our best, we have to let go," my friend went on to say. "Disappointments often prove, in 20/20 hindsight, to be protections in disguise. That was confirmed in my own case, and I have seen it many times since.

"Willfulness is never the way," she concluded. "And our plans are not always the best plans. Let your plans go, and watch what unfolds."

Of course, what my friend said proved true. Ran went on, happily improvising his way into the future. And in continuing my efforts to build the Dance Department, I employed the best of what he had shared with me. Now, thirty years later, everything I feared lost has returned to us both in forms far richer for the separate paths we took.

POLLYANNA AND 'PLAYING GOD'

Wonder is not a Pollyanna stance,
not a denial of reality;
wonder is an acknowledgement
of the power of the mind to transform.

~ Christina Baldwin

Over time and with much practice, we gain confidence in our ability to improvise our way through trying circumstances. This confidence, however, should not to be confused with a Pollyanna attitude.

Such an attitude is not listening. In fact, it is just the opposite. A subtle disguise for fear, this mindset is not attentive to what is happening in and around us, and leaves us unprepared to handle the dangers and difficulties that present themselves.

We must detect fear in thought to be able to address it. We cannot sweep it under the rug. We can expect improvisation to lead us to the best solution only if we are willing to listen, to pay attention; and a Pollyanna attitude towards fear will prevent that.

Akin to this attitude is what we call 'playing God,' a form of willfulness, impelled by fear and often hidden under the guise of 'positive thinking.' Here, instead of listening, we subtly attempt to outline and direct events according to our own limited perspectives and desires.

Improvisation is the very reverse of playing God. It is equally the reverse of worshiping our fears. Improvisation is laying down our fears and willful desires and trusting the listening process to unfold the ideas we need in any circumstance.

Fearful thoughts sometimes suggest that we will be safer, happier, or more successful if we specifically prescribe the forms in which we want things to work out. But fear is not the creative resource that listening is. Instead of opening us up to possibilities of which we never dreamed, fear closes down our receptivity to the unimagined, and limits our horizons.

Both Pollyanna and playing God are subtle traps of fear. Fear handles us if we do not detect and handle it. But once we are willing to face and address fear, we can trust the improvisational mind to guide us to the most appropriate actions and imaginative solutions.

Addressing Fear in Improvisation

What is always speaking silently is the body.

~ Norman O. Brown

Fear never makes good dances or good life practice; only fear-free listening does. In our *Creative Listening* workshops, once we detect fear in any of its guises, we address that fear through safe improvisational exercises and structures.

Before we can create such structures, however, we must be able to translate thought into movement and movement into thought. One way of doing this is to view basic elements of movement composition – space, time, weight, shape – as *metaphors*.

In the following examples, we see how these four elements invite the formation of concrete approaches to identifying and addressing fear through movement:

> **Space** – An improviser may exhibit fear by routinely withdrawing spatially from others, or by habitually making blind, headlong physical contact. Improvisational exercises, which lead to an exploration of both spatial distance and proximity, can make conscious the fear driving these tendencies and offer alternatives to counteract it.

> **Time** – Fear in the form of numbness may be expressed in a habitual, monotonous moderation of speed in movement. Conversely, fear may appear as hyper-busyness evidenced by mindless, scattered, flurried movement. In either case, requiring conscious variations in speed can bring these guises of fear to the improviser's attention and suggest options that offset them.

> **Weight** – An improviser's fear of commitment or inability to trust may appear as reluctance to give weight to another

person. On the other hand, fear expressed as inappropriate dependency may manifest in continually surrendering passive (dead) weight to another. Becoming aware of the feelings behind the behavior, and learning how both to give and take weight, begins to dissipate these manifestations of fear.

Shape – Specific shapes or postures to which improvisers unconsciously and repetitively revert usually indicate a cessation of listening and the presence of fear. Bringing these shapes and their specific mental or emotional content to the dancer's conscious awareness through koans and counter-koans, for instance, can go a long way towards addressing and dissolving the fear that habitual shapes signify.

DISTINGUISHING FEAR FROM SELF

We become what we think of ourselves.

~ Abraham Joshua Heschel

It is crucial in improvisation, as well as in life, to *identify* fear in our consciousness, but not to identify *with* it. Fear is not our selfhood or mind, but an imposition upon it. We are not responsible for the thoughts and feelings that come to us, only what we do with them.

As performers, we take an observer or audience perspective on our thoughts and acts, including every fear we experience. By regarding these fears with a degree of objectivity, we gain distance on them.

This self-awareness provides perspective, a sense of separation between our selves and our fear-based thoughts. This distance can help us to distinguish our selves from the fear, so that it no longer overpowers and engulfs us.

When fears arise in a dance, we detect them. We feel the fear, but from our 'observer' perspective are not subsumed by it. In this frame of mind, we are able consciously to discern the fears and then *perform them*, instead of unconsciously *acting them out*. Although we may make movement choices that symbolically represent the presence of fear, fear is not actively driving our thoughts or directing the dance.

If we fail to listen, undetected fear can control us. For example, fear in the form of anger or bullying may appear in an improvisation when one improviser employs superior physical strength over others in order to muscle the improvisation in a direction of his or her choice. This is literally *acting out* superior strength, not *performing* or *portraying* superior strength.

Performing consciously embodies and conveys an idea. *Acting out* unconsciously allows fear to control thought and action.

Acting out is mindless, whatever form it takes, and has the almost inevitable result of deadening the dance and its potential for creativity and surprise. *Performing*, on the other hand, requires listening without fear, turning fearful impulses into creative fodder, even a bit of wisdom. It connects individuals with one another and creatively enlivens them.

The improvisational practice of detecting fear and distinguishing it from the individual prepares us, in a degree, to successfully apply this same healing and revitalizing process in our daily lives, either when alone or when interacting with others.

FEAR IN OUR INTERACTIONS WITH OTHERS

But let patience have her perfect work,
that ye may be perfect and entire,
wanting nothing.

~ Saint James

Chery: [Michael] *was a very bright, energetic, and mischievous student. I liked him right away. He was intellectually curious and always questioning. In virtually every conversation with me, he took the role of devil's advocate. There was very little I could say that Michael did not challenge.*

The first day of class, I informed my students of a few preliminary rules: never wear shoes into the dance studio, as the studio floor was to be kept pristine; but remember to bring in valuables, such as watches and wallets, and not leave them unattended in the dressing rooms. Michael promptly got up, left the studio, and reentered, carrying his bicycle on his shoulder.

I greatly enjoyed his humor and his challenge. After all, having a questioning mind is what being a student is all about. But there was an element of disruptiveness in Michael's behavior that affected the class, and I knew I had to address this.

Soon, I found occasion for a private conference with Michael. I expressed my appreciation for the liveliness of his mind and his active engagement in the course. "But," I said, "I feel it is only fair to warn you, when it comes to any contest between us, I will always win. I don't try to; I just can't help it." I had his attention.

Then I cited a poem by early 20th century poet Edwin Markham, that my father had taught me:

> *He drew a circle that shut me out –*
> *Heretic, rebel, a thing to flout.*
> *But Love and I had the wit to win.*
> *We drew a circle that took him in.*

"You can knock yourself out contesting me," I told him, "but I will win every match. I will always draw a circle to take you in."

Michael sat silent for several moments, considering this. Then he said, "My mother died when I was thirteen."

And that was the end of the contest.

Most hostile behavior or acting out, no matter where or how it appears, is rooted in fear. Unrecognized fear engenders an unwillingness, if not an inability, to listen and causes breakdowns in communication. Whenever hostility arises in improvisation or in life, it is imperative that we *recognize* fear is operating.

Only with this recognition, can we choose *not to react*. To remain calm in the midst of conflict, it is important not to take the words or actions of fearful individuals personally. Most of the time, their behavior has very little to do with us.

Looking behind the behavior to its origin, we can more easily distinguish fear from person, and person from behavior. Now we have gained the space *to listen* – to observe, to pay attention, to watch.

Our primary charge in a hostile situation is to be aware of what is happening both within and around us; to be alert to, but unaffected by, fear. To do this, it is vital that we neither identify with fear in ourselves, nor take offense at the fearfully driven behavior of others.

If we work on the assumption that fear is something we or others feel, *not who or what we are*, then we need only discover whence the fear originates in order to unmask it as fear and neutralize its negative effects.

After we have assessed the situation with this kind of perspective and clarity, we will be able to move on, *to act* rather than react. Acting preserves our power and independence in our interactions with others. Reacting may feel powerful, but it is always a sign that we have lost self-control.

THE DISCIPLINE OF LISTENING

You never conquer the mountain.
You conquer yourself,
your doubts and fears.

~ Jim Whittaker,
the first American
to climb Mt. Everest

As counter-intuitive as this may seem, being fearful is never a necessity, no matter what the circumstances. It has no inherent authority over us or anyone else.

Once uncovered and distinguished from ourselves and others, the power of fear in its myriad disguises is compromised, and its effects diffused. It can no longer operate as an undetected influence to control thought and action, blocking our receptivity to new ideas.

By listening, we disallow fear's hypnotic claim to dominate thought. And in so doing, we gain all the protective 'survival' elements fear is so often believed to provide – *alertness, awakeness, awareness* – without incurring any of its liabilities.

Faced with a frightening situation, we may find it momentarily difficult to let go of fear and trust the act of listening to reveal a solution. Here is where discipline, practice, and experience come into play.

Discipline allows us to turn from the overpowering images fear presents and, instead, focus on listening. The more we practice listening, the more readily available it will be, as success steadily increases our willingness to turn thought quickly and confidently in this direction.

Chery: Sometimes we share an insight with another person. We, ourselves, then forget it altogether, while it remains with the other for a lifetime. Such was the case with a three-part Chinese riddle that Ran relayed to me thirty years ago: How can we hold water, fire, and wind in paper?

As years went by, I recalled only two of the answers. When Ran and I sat down to write this book, I eagerly quizzed him for the answer I had long forgotten, but discovered he had no memory even of the question.

For several months, I struggled to remember the missing answer without success. One night, I finally gave up. Putting into practice my own prescription, I just let go and listened.

In the silence that followed, doubt began to creep in. Does listening really work? Maybe it doesn't, after all. Can I really expect an answer to come to me after such a span of years?

Then this realization came: There is no time in the improvisational mind; it is always in the eternal present. With that message, my anxiety subsided. And within minutes, an answer appeared.

I have no way of knowing whether these were the original answers, but here are the three I now had: We can capture water in a straw, fire in a Chinese lantern, and wind in a fan.

In the face of anxiety or fear, the essential thing is to regain our mental balance – to focus on listening – and not succumb to fear's claims for attention.

No matter how commanding it may seem, fear is not, by and large, constructive. Beyond alerting us to pay attention, its effect is generally to freeze or distract thought and hinder our receptivity, ingenuity, and creative imagination.

GRATITUDE

The songbird sings before the dawn.

~ Myrtle Smyth

More often than not, just reminding ourselves to listen is all we need to gain dominion over fear. There are times, however, when fear simply engulfs us, even in the pettiest of circumstances.

Whenever we are feeling overwhelmed, a shift in our mental standpoint from fear to gratitude can help us regain our footing. Gratitude for any past or present good, no matter how small, tends to lift and release us from fixation on our distress over the current situation and create space to listen.

In particular, remembering former situations – ones where the practice of listening revealed solutions in unexpected, improbable, even ingenious ways – strengthens our confidence in the improvisational process and helps break the hold of fear, the principal impediment to our creativity.

Grateful appreciation directs thought toward an expectation of success, without presupposing the exact outcome. To anticipate the success of a performance piece or project, even before its beginning, may appear to be placing the cart before the horse, but this change of focus serves to shift the balance of our attention from fear to receptivity, and from receptivity to creativity.

Ran: Recently, I was participating in a book discussion group at the local library. Ten minutes after the discussion began, [Ethan] came in late, complaining that he hadn't even had dinner yet. With a flourish, he noisily opened his pizza carton and dug in.

Within a few minutes, Ethan jumped into the conversation, confessed he had not read the book, and then commenced to lecture the group for over a quarter of an hour on everything he knew about the general topic.

At first, I only felt annoyed. But as the minutes dragged on, my anger and frustration grew until I completely shut down. All around, eyeballs rolled in expressions of impatience and boredom, and all I could think was how much I wanted to stuff Ethan's pizza down his throat.

From long experience, I knew I should be listening and trusting the improvisational process, but I had lost all motivation to try. I felt no respect for Ethan, and so, no interest in listening to him. He unknowingly had pushed one of my 'hot buttons,' my own fear of offending in exactly the same way.

Finally, I admitted to myself what was happening, and my attention shifted. I recalled with gratitude similar situations in which I had grown hard-hearted and then recovered my sense of compassion.

Now, I began to look for things I could respect about Ethan. I noted that he was obviously well educated and well spoken, possessed an earnest concern for the topic, and seemed genuinely eager to contribute to the discussion.

Gradually, my agitation subsided. The fear hidden under my impatience dissolved and I began to listen. Soon, I recognized how what Ethan was saying did relate to our subject, and I became genuinely interested.

Picking up on Ethan's thread, I spoke up. Underlining his theme, I connected it to the previous on-going discussion about the book. Eyes around the room came back into focus, and the conversation again took off.

Listening is the improviser's creative power. Whichever way we access that listening state – either by detecting fear, distinguishing it from self, and disallowing its domination through the discipline of listening, or simply by turning our focus from fear to gratitude – we can learn progressively to free the improvisational mind to attend, unobstructed, the still, small voice of creativity.

THE IMPROVISATIONAL MIND

If you love to listen
you will gain knowledge,
and if you pay attention
you will become wise.

~ Ben Sira

The improvisational mind entails a balance of inner and outer awareness.

It involves not just listening, but a three-dimensional state of listening: paying attention simultaneously to self, others, and the environment.

We use the word 'listening' deliberately to distinguish it as a mental process from that of thinking. And this distinction is an important one, because, in fact, the improvisational mind cannot be accessed by thinking, but by listening only.

Listening implies an openness of mind, a state free of prejudice and fully alert to the present. It connotes willingness rather than willfulness and includes qualities such as receptivity, vigilance, expectancy, flexibility, vitality, trust, poise, patience, empathy, and compassion. This is the creative state.

To clarify our terms, *the act* of listening without fear is referred to here as *creative listening* and *the state* of listening without fear, as *the improvisational mind*.

In sports, this alert, relaxed mental state is called 'being in the zone.' When we are in the zone, we are present to whatever is happening here and now.

In this mentality, there are no mistakes. If we stumble, the stumble becomes the dance. Discerning, but not judgmental, the improvisational mind pays attention with interest and curiosity to whatever transpires.

43

No Mistakes

Do not fear mistakes.
There are none.

~ Miles Davis

Chery: "You mean there are no mistakes? There are no rules? Anything goes?"
Jonathan was alarmed. This was the first day of my improvisation course at
Wesleyan, and I had just given the class their first directives.

"I take that back," I responded. "There are mistakes. You are absolutely prohibited
*from doing anything you don't **feel** like doing." The class laughed.*

But Jonathan's concern was not allayed. "Isn't there any right or wrong?" he pressed.

"To cease to listen," I responded more soberly, "to let fear overcome your atten-
*tion, that is the one mistake you can make. Anything **else** goes."*

Jonathan's questions occasioned a vital discussion in class that day. I maintained
that improvisation is not self-indulgence, as some critics suggest, but a highly
disciplined practice.

As the class soon discovered for themselves, the improviser must remain keenly
attuned both inwardly and outwardly, with strict attentiveness to – and yet no
personal direction of – self, others, and events.

What explicitly does not 'go' in improvisation are mindlessness and fear.
And the endeavor to eliminate these two factors – to maintain perpetually
an improvisational state of mind – provides us with lifetime employment.

Indeed, as a postscript to the story above, Jonathan soon proved an exceptional improviser and went on to become a much-loved and esteemed
rabbi. When he talks of his life's work today, he describes it as "all improvisation – listening without fear."

Chery & Ran: More recently, the question of 'mistakes' surfaced in a Creative
Listening workshop we were leading. One dancer in a large group piece sank to a

position on the floor where she remained, her vision of the other dancers entirely obscured. A second dancer, rapidly backing up, fell over her and hit his head soundly on the floor.

The performers froze, as everyone turned to see. The fallen dancer was fine, but others were momentarily shaken. One leaned down and lifted the fallen dancer's head.

Later, as the group discussed the incident, questions arose. "You say there are no mistakes in improvisation, but wasn't this fall a mistake? Wasn't walking backwards rapidly and blindly a mistake? Especially in a dance with a large cast, wasn't remaining in a crouched position with one's vision blocked a mistake?"

The group gradually came to the conclusion that the more balanced our awareness of self, other, and environment, the better. "We have a perpetual responsibility as improvisers to be as alert as possible at every moment, not only to ourselves, but to everything around us," they decided.

As the discussion continued, questions progressed to a deeper level. "Is the improvisational mind impossible to sustain when a performance suddenly shifts into 'real life,' as with this fall? Can we reasonably expect to remain fearless and alert then?"

The performer who had rushed to lift the head of the fallen dancer worried, "What if there had been a serious injury? Wasn't my precipitous response a real-life mistake?"

In performance as in life, if we lose our listening, we lose our presence of mind. The group determined that, if an event occurs in a workshop setting where it appears someone might be hurt, it would be right to pause and check before proceeding with the piece.

"In such a moment, we must drop to another level of awareness, another level of improvisation," they said, "from 'performance improvisation' to 'real-life improvisation.' But regardless of what level we are operating on, we must resist letting fear render us mindless."

At this point, reflecting back on the piece just performed, we realized we had witnessed the paradigm for action we were seeking. With hardly a pause, the fallen dancer had rolled to standing, and then bent backwards gracefully over the crouched woman.

Recapitulating his original fall in slow motion, he had reiterated and developed the theme of that startling event, this time with full awareness of his surroundings. Instead of ignoring the fall, he had integrated it into the ongoing dance and transformed his stumble into an occasion for creativity.

"Even if we do succumb to fear in improvisation or in life," the group concluded, "a real-life mistake can only be defined as that experience where we fail, either immediately or upon later reflection, to recover our listening state, integrate the incident, and move on."

In other words, any untoward experience through which we do not learn can legitimately be considered a mistake. But that 'mistake' is determined not by the act or experience itself, but by how we do or do not listen to what has happened *after the fact.*

What gets in the way of listening after the fact? Shock, pride, self-condemnation, dishonesty – any form of fear. Humbly trusting the process of listening to generate our next steps, we can turn from fear and concern for self or others, move forward, and learn from our experience.

MINDFULNESS

For precept must be upon precept,
precept upon precept;
line upon line, line upon line;
here a little, and there a little.

~ Isaiah

We approach the improvisational mind as an ideal type to which we aspire. Realizing our creative potential through its practice is a step-by-step learning process that demands moment-by-moment attention and mindfulness.

Though at first we may seldom fully achieve this state, to the degree that we practice the discipline of listening, we will become increasingly less vulnerable to fear and consistently more creative.

Chery: *From the very beginning, the circumstances were terrifying. As a twenty-year-old still in college, I was hired to introduce dance into the curriculum at Wesleyan University at a time when Wesleyan was still an all male institution.*

For my first six years, I taught as a non-tenure-track faculty. So it was twelve years, not the usual six, before my tenure case came up for consideration.

All along, the dance program had been growing. But the future of dance at Wesleyan was far from assured. Only if I were awarded tenure, would dance survive. Otherwise, the program would most likely disappear.

As a subject of academic study, dance in the 1970s was still viewed with deep suspicion by many in the administration and faculty, and hot debate surrounded this tenure case. But finally, after my passing every other test, tenure came down to whether my artistic skill measured up.

The problem was this: My creative work primarily revolved around Sonomama, *which neither I nor anyone else directed. So even if the company as a whole was deemed successful, questions lingered in the minds of some as to whether I, on my own, had convincingly demonstrated the requisite level of artistic excellence.*

Several visiting committees of dance professionals reviewed my work and voiced their approval. But as a large future curricular and financial commitment for Wesleyan rode upon this decision, the President decided he would invite a friend whom he could trust, the Head of the National Endowment for the Arts, to come and help him make his final assessment.

To the dance faculty's knowledge, the President had never attended a dance concert on campus in the program's history. There was much trepidation over what he would think of an improvisational art form, which at that time was still decidedly avant-garde.

As our little band of performers huddled backstage before the concert, we reminded ourselves how important trust and humility were to accessing the improvisational mind. In a burst of spontaneous playfulness, we began to sing the Shaker song, "'Tis a gift to be simple, 'Tis a gift to be free, 'Tis a gift to come down where we ought to be." And with that, we walked out onstage and into our unscripted performance.

Since the question the university sought to answer was whether I myself possessed clear talent, it was on the concert's one improvisational structure where each dancer performed a solo that the weight of the whole case seemed to fall that night. One single dance.

In this structure, the only pre-set directive was for the first dancer to assume any position onstage he or she chose and from there to improvise a solo. Whatever the final position of that dance happened to be, became the beginning position for the next soloist, and so on through the whole company.

Beginning positions are always critical. They, more than any one thing, determine the direction of a dance. On this particular evening, it just fell out that I was the last performer in the solo series. As I prepared to take my place, I realized with horror the position in which the previous dancer had ended. He was lying spread eagle, face down on the floor.

I can still remember the parquet floor as I lay on my belly awaiting inspiration – hey, any impulse at all! – to move. The weight of what rested on my shoulders – the lives my success or failure would impact; the dreams for the department itself, its vision and promise; even the place of dance in the larger academic mission, which each of my dance colleagues had so hoped to further – all this pressed down upon me then, as if funneled into one single point in space and time.

The little ditty, "'Tis a gift to be simple," floated into my mind. I recalled the countless improvisations I had performed and witnessed. I knew well that no matter how hopelessly small and insignificant an impulse or intuition seemed, if it came from listening, it would be alive to the moment. I also knew that, if instead, I made something up, no matter how technically impressive, it would be instantly forgettable.

So I waited. And as I waited, a feeling of gratitude unexpectedly entered my consciousness. Gratitude simply that at long last this moment had arrived, that after years of labor and love, dance at the university had finally come to this point of serious consideration.

My thought began to expand, reaching out to those around me. Suddenly, I felt grateful to all the people in the audience who, through their presence, were giving me this precious opportunity – to my students and my colleagues, to the president and his friend. But most of all I felt grateful that through work with Sonomama *I had glimpsed the creative power of listening … and that listening was all I had to do.*

I must have moved, because I remember at the end of the dance the beaming faces, the cheers, the applause. But most of all, I remember the pure peace and effortlessness I felt, watching the dance emerge.

A colleague, recently recalling this event twenty-five years later, said, "Oh, I remember that dance clear as day. You began flat on your face. But you ended upright, facing us all. Sinking to your knees, you reached out your arms as if to embrace the whole world."

RECEPTIVITY

*The smartest way to work
is to not quite know
what you're doing.*

~ Tibor Kalman

How do we enter the improvisational mind – and stay there? Addressing this question is what our practice is all about. It begins with emptying consciousness of fear and any willful plans or designs of our own, and then opening ourselves expectantly to receive whatever comes.

In this receptive state, we become awake to the *present* in all of its aspects: our own thoughts, feelings, and intuitions; the impressions of shapes, sounds, and movements made by others in the space; and beyond that, the nature of our environment – the immediate physical surroundings and even the larger social, political, or cultural context.

There is no planning ahead in the improvisational state. Focused entirely upon what is happening now, we are incapable of anxiety over what might happen next.

Chery: Recently, I was lifting weights at my local gym. A friend, who was in the midst of an aerobics class, caught my eye and dashed out to greet me.

"I can only talk a moment," Lynn said breathlessly, grabbing both my hands. "I have to get back to class. But I had a dream last night and you were in it."

The dream she recounted was this: The two of us were walking toward our car, when we came upon a river that blocked our way. My friend and I stood on the riverbank, stymied.

At first, all we were aware of was the obstruction the river presented. But looking closer, we saw that the water was teeming with a magnificent array of brilliantly colored sea creatures, moving fluidly in and out and among one another with indescribable beauty.

The thwarted plans which a moment before had consumed our thoughts were for-gotten. A glorious, all-absorbing spectacle lay at our feet. All that mattered – the pure joy of life – was here and now!

The improvisational mind always exists in the unhurried, timeless present. One of the most distinctive qualities of the listening state is its effortless-ness and ease. Once we have achieved this state, there is no sense of worry about the future or past, no strain, no struggle.

As improvisers, we simply embody in our movements the ideas and intu-itions that arise in consciousness moment by moment. It is almost as effort-less as a reflection in a mirror. Listening does not impose on any situation, but merely reflects what is happening in the present.

This listening state of mind is pure receptivity. For most adults, used to being responsible and taking control, accessing the improvisational mind involves a significant mental shift. It requires letting go of the reins, taking a back seat, and 'watching' the dance unfold.

This is not to imply that creative listening is passive. Far from it! The vigilance required to maintain a balanced awareness of self, others, and the environment, and to respond by following through with action, makes the listening process highly charged with focus and energy.

Furthermore, it would be naive to imagine that both performer and observer are not actively involved in shaping their perceptions. What any of us actually hears is determined in part by the lens of our own consciousness – our most fundamental view of the nature of reality itself, and beyond that, our values, assumptions, prejudices, even what we had for lunch.

Listening is an active, not a passive state, involving concentration, perception, and interpretation. But most of all, it requires an openness to receive and reflect everything 'just as it is' (*sonomama*).

INTUITION

We cannot direct the wind,
but we can adjust the sails.

~ Anonymous

Intuition plays a dominant role in creativity. This is not to say that other processes of the conscious mind are absent. However, they operate as servants, not masters.

For example, to be in the zone, athletes must, to a degree, disengage their intellects from their actions. If too mentally directive or willful, an athlete loses his or her touch.

Like athletes, artists who are too self-conscious, or who lead predominantly with their intellects or wills, also lose touch with their intuition. In such instances, their work is apt to become studied and lifeless.

Whether artist, athlete, or average Joe, we must trust our intuition in order to respond aptly and adeptly to the unrehearsed present. Instead of attempting to direct the situation and control the outcome, learning to listen and follow our intuitive leadings is our answer to uncertainty.

Ran: I began playing baseball in the fourth grade. As a catcher, my biggest challenge came when an opposing player made it to first base. I knew that the runner's next move would be an immediate attempt to steal second.

In anxious anticipation, I would mentally rehearse my throw to second base. Since I was barely able to fling the ball that far, let alone hit the bag, by the time the runner attempted to steal, my mind was overrun with fear.

The harder I tried to will a perfect throw, the worse things got. Most of the time, my peg to second ended up in center field. More often than not, I hit my own pitcher square in the back.

Gradually, I learned that the only chance I had to get the runner out was to stop anticipating the worst. I had to tell myself that I could make the play, and then throw with my body, not my head.

We may wish to believe otherwise; but, ultimately, we must confront the fact that we do not control life. The only true certainty we have at our command is our ability to practice the improvisational mind.

COUNTER-INTUITION

When I become enlightened,
my mind will be the last to know.

~ Catherine Royce

Besides its *intuitive* nature, another striking feature of creativity is its *counter-intuitive* nature. Creative thinking is instinctively intelligent, but very often this intelligence does not appear rational or commonsensical.

'Intuitive perception' connotes immediate apprehension, direct knowledge or cognition that, in coming to its conclusions, bypasses the more methodical processes of logic or reason. 'Counter-intuitive perception' implies a similarly shrewd discernment, but one that expressly appears illogical or irrational, the direct opposite of commonsense.

Both intuition and counter-intuition are sources of insight characteristic of improvisation and, indeed, of most creative endeavors.

Chery: From the age of five into my teenage years, I was enrolled in a local dance school run by Betty Jane Dittmar, a teacher with exceptional creative vision in arts education.

*One summer at her Strawberry Hill Center for Creative Arts, Betty Jane presented what appeared to be a counter-intuitive assignment in poetry. Her directions: "Don't think about what to write or how to write it. Just **listen** and write down whatever comes. Just be the scribe."*

As one who endlessly labored over writing assignments, I had no faith whatsoever that this would work. But I obeyed. I made no effort to create anything; I just listened.

Suddenly, fresh, vivid images came directly to mind, and the necessary words came with them. The little haiku-like poems that resulted were surprisingly arresting, and rich in multi-layered meanings.

It required humility and courage to let go of my usual 'having to do it myself' attitude. It demanded patience to wait and listen, and it took trust to follow so counter-intuitive an approach. But one after another, the ideas came.

Looking back, it was the first time I remember consciously losing my mind in order to find it.

The counter-intuitive quality of the creative mentality may be one of the reasons that the teaching of creativity seems so elusive to academia with its traditional emphasis on memory, logic, and reason. The current focus in secondary education on uniform testing and away from flexibility and invention only reinforces this traditional bias.

Yet, creative thinking is an essential element in most professions, as well as everyday life. And improvisation is undeniably one of the best venues for its exploration and practice.

Intuition vs. Impulsiveness

And thine ears shall hear a word behind thee, saying,
this is the way, walk ye in it,
when ye turn to the right hand,
and when ye turn to the left.

~ Isaiah

When intuition is guiding us, we experience a sense of being *impelled*.

At some point, anyone who attempts to follow the leadings of intuition questions whether this urge actually is intuition, or just foolish impulsiveness. How is it possible to tell the difference?

We know of no foolproof method. Only with personal experience and considerable feedback from outside observers does the improviser begin to distinguish the genuine from the counterfeit. But when our actions feel or appear forced, willfully urgent, frightened, or inauthentic, these are signs we have lost our way.

If doubting the wisdom of an impulse, we can always take a step in that direction and see what happens. If a door opens, we can take another step or two and listen again. If, on the other hand, the way seems to close, then we must wait, watch, and listen for an opening in another direction.

Sometimes we listen and hear nothing. When this happens, it usually indicates that fear or its derivative, willfulness, is in operation. Intuition is a remarkable source of intelligence, but it eludes us if our motive is to get or direct our own way.

A receptive attitude and a willingness to self-correct – to change course with yielding humility and grace – are necessary both to hear and to follow intuition. Naturally, this is not always easy. When we do follow our intuition, however, its uncanny wisdom can transform an otherwise ordinary circumstance into an extraordinary life experience.

Chery: The Office of Admissions at Wesleyan held annual events, designed to introduce and welcome prospective students and their parents to campus. Representatives from each of the arts gave short talks on their educational programs.

One year, reflecting yet again on what I would say, I remembered a recent article in U.S. News and World Report.[1] *The piece explored the transformative effect of the arts in education, focusing particularly on inner city schools.*

The authors of the article concluded:

> *Ultimately, the greatest value of the arts may be that they offer children the means to envision other worlds, to know that they can transform reality with the exercise of their own creative will. For kids whose horizons extend no further than the dead ends of the inner city, that leap of imagination can be critical.*

The thought occurred to me that the main points of my talk could be illustrated by paraphrasing one of the teachers interviewed in this article. Since it was late when I turned to the task of framing my presentation, I just jotted down a few notes and fell exhausted into bed.

As I drifted off to sleep, a small but distinct intuition came to me to retrieve the article from my files and quote, not just paraphrase, the teacher's comments. "Oh, no," I thought. "Do I really have to crawl out of bed and do this? What difference will it make? Who will care?" Gently, the intuition persisted.

---

1   Miriam Horn with Jill Sieder, "Looking for a Renaissance: The Campaign to Revive Education in the Arts," in *U.S. News and World Report* March 30, 1992, pp. 52-54.

After arguing with myself for some time, finally I paused and listened. It came to me then that the occasion of this talk was really an important opportunity. All that lies within the arts is invaluable to the academic experience of any young person. The chance to share in this experience is, after all, what I was giving my whole life for. It was worth doing right.

The next day, along with other arts faculty, I gave my little presentation. Afterwards, a number of students and parents came up to speak with me. The article had hit home.

When everyone else had cleared away, a woman and her husband approached. Their son was considering Wesleyan, they said. They felt a deep alliance between what I had portrayed as the mission of the Dance Department and their own interests.

"You see, I am an art teacher, myself," the woman explained. "The one you quoted in the article."

BALANCE OF INNER AND OUTER

*Somewhere we know
that, without silence,
words lose their meaning;
that, without listening,
speaking no longer heals;
that, without distance,
closeness cannot cure.*

~ Henri Nouwen

Accessing the improvisational mind involves a reorientation for most adults, but this state of mind is not itself disoriented. Quite the opposite: it is the synchronization of our internal and external orientations.

The improvisational mind requires the simultaneous presence of both an inner and outer awareness – an awareness of self, of the others with whom we are interacting, and of the larger context or environment.

In movement improvisation, context may include the space in which we are performing, specifically any physical characteristics of that space and any objects therein. It may also include persons beyond the stage space, such as an audience.

Even farther afield, context may incorporate purely mental elements, such as the rules of the game, the larger culture in which we are performing, however that may be defined, or the expectations of the community in which we are situated.

Maintaining an on-going inner and outer integration of awareness is an essential prerequisite to creativity. Some people listen better to themselves than to others. Conversely, some listen better to others, or external circumstances, than to themselves. But the trick, in any case, is to sustain a balance between the two foci. To accomplish and maintain this integration requires constant vigilance and practice.

Ran: One day, a young woman, [Sharon], contacted me for some personal counseling. After many heart surgeries, her only child had died in infancy.

It was now almost a year since [Brian's] death, yet Sharon was so haunted by his memory that she was unable to respond to her husband or resume her vocation as a graphic artist. Her husband had become exasperated with her, and she feared she was losing him, too.

After several sessions with no apparent progress, I proposed that our next meeting be held in Sharon's home. This suggestion was only the result of a vague notion I had that a change of venue might get us moving again.

On arriving at her house, I found a perfectly appointed nursery, arranged as if the baby's return were imminent. Sharon had changed nothing since Brian's death. She could not bring herself to let go of a single object associated with her son.

After several more meetings, the grieving mother came to the conclusion that, to regain her balance, she would have to give up the bulk of her baby's belongings. She would keep a few things, but only what would fit into the baby's toy box.

Sharon imaginatively devised a plan by which she would give items away one at a time to people who could use them. As a result, she made contact with dozens of community members, and the items became a means of transferring her love for Brian to the children of others.

Shortly after the completion of this labor of love, she ended her marriage and left town. She returned to school for additional training and soon was working productively as a graphic artist.

A year or two later, I received a packet of hand-painted Christmas tree ornaments and a letter. The pain was still there, Sharon wrote, but it had eased. She felt once again among the living. Her creative energies had returned, and she was now moving on.

As Sharon discovered, if we become lost within ourselves, we disconnect from the activities and concerns of those around us. Likewise, if we become enmeshed in external events, we lose touch with the immediacy of our own impulses and intuitions. Neither extreme, if it persists over time, generates good improvisations – in art or in life.

DYNAMIC BALANCE

Balance is not stillness, but constant motion.

~ Anonymous

We are speaking of 'balance' as the integration of inner and outer awareness, where a relaxed but focused mind is attained and a safe but stimulating atmosphere fostered. However, the term 'balance' can be misleading.

What is meant here is not a stable state of fifty percent inner-awareness and fifty percent outer-awareness. Such a state is very rare. What we are describing is rather a continuous, often rapid, 'mental tacking' between attention to inner impulses and outer stimuli.

The 'Walkaround' is an improvisational structure with which we begin every workshop. It is designed to prepare dancers to improvise, and it does so by focusing on this mental tacking, the primary skill needed to see and take full advantage of our internal and external options for action, and to move creatively among them.

In the 'Walkaround,' dancers begin by standing on the perimeter of the performing space. They are directed to close their eyes, feel the soles of their feet on the floor, extend their spines through the crown of their heads, and center their weight in their hips an inch or two below their navels.

They then open their eyes, relax their gaze, and establish their peripheral vision to take in the whole room. As a group, they simultaneously inhale deeply, and on the exhale, enter the space walking.

Throughout the piece, all that the performers do is walk, weaving in and around one another. Without losing a sense of centeredness in their legs and hips, they maintain their peripheral vision, even to the point of imagining they can see behind themselves as if by radar.

Eventually, improvisers learn to go with the flow of the whole group without losing their own centeredness. They remain aware of their individual responses, while being carried by the currents of movement around them, like a surfer riding a wave.

Concerted individual and group practice is required, but when an inner and outer balance is achieved and sustained, performers and audience alike experience an uplifting sense of freedom, surprise, and harmony, something akin to a spontaneous symphony.

INSTABILITY

I travel a lot;
I hate having my life disrupted
by routine.

~ Caskie Stinnett

Creativity is very often impelled by mental or situational crises and instability. As an asymmetrical shape lends itself more readily to motion than a symmetrical one, so an unstable mental state or external situation is more likely to invite innovation than a stable one.

How we respond to unstable conditions is what determines their outcome. We can see unsettled situations as turmoil and destruction, or we can take them as creative opportunities. Balancing inner and outer awareness is the key to transforming situational instability into a creative wellspring.

Chery: After earning his M.S. in geophysics, my brother accepted employment with an oil company. In 1986, when oil prices crashed, he lost his job and virtually everything he owned.

That Thanksgiving at a family gathering, Thor and I had a chance to talk, and I sought to lift his spirits. "You have never been, and probably will never be again, so free," I told him. "You have no strings. You can totally 'blue-sky.' Now is the moment to ask where you want to throw the weight of your life on this earth for the time you have left."

Thor reflected silently for a while. Then without preliminary explanation, he told me this story: "When I was ten, our Boy Scout troop went on a camping trip to Fox, a rural Alaskan village. We pitched our tents next to a small artesian spring.

"I will never forget that water," he said. "It was so pure, all it tasted was cold. I think if I had the power to do anything, I would bring water like that to the whole earth."

That quiet realization was the turning point. Not long after, Thor accepted a job with the National Oceanographic and Atmospheric Administration (NOAA). In this position, he received specific training in pollution control.

Three years later, he was back in Alaska, now working for the Environmental Protection Agency (EPA), very happily married, and with his first child on the way. He was not six months into his job when a tanker, the Exxon Valdez, made national headlines by running aground in Prince Williams Sound.

Almost overnight, Thor found himself on the scene, assigned to cleaning up the pristine waters he so prized in the largest oil spill in the history of the United States.

Whether reassessing our direction in life or simply seeking to develop our creativity, upheaval and unrest can be our best allies. They challenge us to respond to life's vicissitudes without losing our own equilibrium and perspective.

Like a quick-moving martial artist or athlete, it is an inward sense of calm and centeredness that allows us to make use of a volatile situation in order to achieve optimal outward mobility and innovation.

VISION

To see a World in a Grain of Sand
And a Heaven in a Wild Flower
Hold Infinity in the palm of your hand,
And Eternity in an hour

~ William Blake

Closely akin to an awareness of inner and outer is an awareness of near and far. If our attention is either too myopic and concrete or too broad, abstract, and theoretical, our creative efforts will suffer.

What produces the most creative results is a balance between attention to details and attention to overview. Sometimes we must step in to engage the specifics immediately confronting us, and sometimes we must step back to grasp the big picture. But ultimately, we cannot afford to remain for long at the extremes, with either nearsighted or farsighted vision.

LETTING GO

People wish to be settled;
only as far as they are unsettled
is there any hope for them.

~ Ralph Waldo Emerson

Dancers and martial artists maintain their physical balance by knowing how to center their bodies – where to focus their attention, where to hold, and where to let go. Such bodily control is best attained by employing principles of physics rather than brute strength. In a metaphoric sense, this lesson is equally applicable to the creative process.

On occasion, we may be tempted to force the creative process through willful, almost brute effort. But at some point, the more we grind, the less we get. At times like these, perhaps counter-intuitively, the secret to enhanced creativity is letting go.

By focusing on the present, we can let go of fears and distractions and center ourselves through listening. This centeredness is the only actual control available to the improvisational mind. It is self-control through inner and outer awareness, as opposed to control over others or over external circumstances.

Self-awareness, balanced with a comprehensive awareness of the larger context, endows the improviser with all the power he or she needs in order to act amidst uncertainty.

In this optimal creative state, the improvisational mind surfs the waves of thought and action. This surfing encompasses a sense of looseness and lightness necessary for rolling with the waves, as well as a sense of centeredness needed to ride them.

No one combats seasickness by attempting to freeze the sea, but some believe it can be overcome by fixing our eye on the horizon, relaxing our bodies, and going with the waves.

In everyday life, as well as in improvisational performance, when faced with fearful change, we often cling to the solid ground of our old ideas, our old scripts. We look to these familiar forms to keep us oriented.

But an alternative approach is to focus on the present for our sense of stability, and then just let go and trust the fluid unfolding of new ideas, the creative process within ourselves.

STRUCTURE

Structures of which we are unaware
hold us prisoner.

~ Peter Senge

We have maintained that the optimal state of mind for engendering creativity is a centered, fear-free state, where we are open to 'going with the flow.' So what role, if any, does 'structure' play in all of this?

The truth is that we are never outside some form of structure. Nothing occurs in a vacuum. There are always contingencies and external constraints to any creative or improvisational act. To the alert listener, these external contexts will function not as distractions or impediments, but as structural elements helping to orient the direction of his or her creative exploration.

One of our important assignments as improvisers is to be as sensitive as possible to whatever environmental circumstances exist in a particular place and time. Then, to create work relevant to that context, the improvisational mind needs only to be set adrift, like a river guided by its banks.

Some people report experiencing their greatest creativity in wide-open, relaxed circumstances, free from external directives or demands. Released from self-consciousness, they let go of their concerns regarding judgment or success.

Others claim they work best under pressure. Externally imposed structure and demands help focus their attention and energy.

Some individuals prefer a tighter structure around a creative project, some a looser one. The degree of tightness or looseness is best determined by how well externally imposed boundaries accomplish two objectives: the reduction of fear and anxiety in the mind of the creator, and the stimulation of his or her thought.

We say a creative project is 'under-structured' when the improviser feels too vulnerable to take risks. The looseness of the guidelines leaves him or her feeling lost, without adequate external points of orientation. We say the project is 'over-structured' when the improviser feels stifled, too constricted by external commands to follow his or her own intuitions.

The desirability of tailoring structures to different individuals is manifest everywhere, from institutional settings to family life. No two people respond to directions, boundaries, and feedback in exactly the same way. In managing personnel, raising children, or creating a dance, both harmony and productivity will be enhanced by sensitivity to individual structural needs.

Chery: Any dancer who encountered Bessie Schönberg, Chair of Dance at Sarah Lawrence College when I was an undergraduate, knows how profoundly she affected her students. There were life-long lessons hidden in the way Bessie taught dance. One such lesson I witnessed occurred when she was advising one of her graduate students, Adinah, on her choreographic project.

Had Adinah been free to cast her own piece, she would undoubtedly have selected two dancers with more similar body types. Now, she was struggling to get Lee and me, different as we were, to perform movement that looked identical. One movement phrase was proving particularly difficult.

In rehearsal one day, Bessie and Adinah watched the two of us perform this phrase repeatedly without success. Finally, Bessie intervened. She directed Lee to think of the outward shape and line of the movement, the clarity of its spatial intent. She directed me to think of its inner motivation, both its physical point of origin and its message. Lee and I tried once again.

As we danced, out of the corner of my eye I saw Bessie and Adinah break into smiles. Contrary directives had produced, they later told us, virtually identical results.

I was dumbfounded at the success of Bessie's approach. How and why had it worked?

"You cannot reach everyone the same way," Bessie explained. "Individual's minds are structured differently. To teach effectively, you have to watch a student closely enough to figure out how her mind works."

LIMINALITY

Anything I've ever done
that ultimately was worthwhile,
initially scared me to death.

~ Betty Bender

In a way, the improvisational mind is analogous to the suspended state of the traveler. The creator, like the traveler, is in liminal space, 'the space between.' This is the wilderness where change happens and creativity is bred. It should come as no surprise, therefore, that many receive their best creative insights traveling on trains or waiting in airports between flights.

In some Native American traditions, the adolescent rite-of-passage is called a 'Vision Quest.' In the tradition of the Australian Aborigines, it is called a 'Walkabout.' These traditional rites involve a shift from an every-day mental state to a liminal state, where thought opens to inspired insight and revelation.

In *Sonomama*, a shadow of these same practices appeared with the 'Walkaround' described above, the first improvisational structure the company created. This structure provided a meditative warm-up, meant to clear the mental decks. It was designed to move performers into a liminal state of enhanced receptivity, from reliance on the known – the safe and habitual – into openness to the unknown.

Upon leaving her position at Wesleyan, Chery found herself propelled into just such a liminal state, a virtual 'Walkaround.'

Chery: I had loved teaching, but after thirty-two years of passionate commitment and intense labor, I sought the peace of an early retirement.

For the first time in memory, I had no plan for my life. My sister, Kristen, reached out with this word of reassurance, "You don't have to accomplish anything else – ever. All you have to do is pay the bills and not go crazy."

Every day I got into my car and drove into the countryside. No destination, no goal. I just followed my intuition, taking any direction I felt like taking.

*It was as if I had prepared all my life to be ready for this – but **was** I ready?*

As I left the university for the last time, my students had sought to reassure me. "Just improvise," they told me. "Like you taught us."

Gulp!

In my first week of freedom, I visited the tiny audio book section of my local library. Two books on Zen stood side by side on the shelf. Both, I remembered with plea-sure, Ran had suggested I read in our seminal days with Sonomama.

I had only time to glance at the books back then. Now I had time for everything! I would pop them into the tape deck of my car and polish them off.

As I traveled through the countryside over the next few days, listening to the tapes, it dawned on me how broadly my work, not only in improvisation but also in the development of the Dance Department, had been affected by these ideas. The discovery was breathtaking. I had to find and contact Ran.

History has such an uncanny way of repeating itself. As it had thirty years before, our collaboration now began again in the wide-open, lost, liminal space of a 'Walkaround.'

LIMINAL CONTEXTS

*Not in his goals
but in his transitions
is man great.*

~ Ralph Waldo Emerson

Although our richest creativity often occurs when we are out of our habit-ual, safe space, this in-between-ness is frightening for many. Transitions are not always pleasant. They are periods of uncertainty, unknowing.

For the improvisational mind, the unknown is full of creative potential.

If we trust it, encountering the unknown can be stress-free and peaceful. We learn during transitions simply to listen, resting in the confidence that listening will disclose and unfold whatever is needed.

How can we foster this relaxed, yet vigilant state? One way is to create our own liminal contexts.

We can stimulate our creativity by exchanging familiar surroundings for unfamiliar ones, choosing circumstances and settings that are new and that disrupt our normal life patterns. We can travel, relocate our work, or enter an isolated place, free from the call of daily demands and routines. Any of these possibilities force us to chance the unknown.

Or we can do just the opposite. Instead of the unfamiliar, we can focus on the familiar. We can relax and let our minds roam by performing physical activity so practiced that it takes only minimal cognitive energy to execute – like driving a car, riding a bike, gardening, or walking. Loosed from the pressures of everyday concerns, our thought can escape, unhindered and playful, into 'blue-sky' territory.

ENTER AND EXIT

They also serve who only stand and wait.

~ John Milton

In our workshops, we artificially produce liminal contexts through an improvisational structure called 'Enter and Exit.' Here dancers spend at least some time just standing offstage, waiting to enter.

Performers in any arena of life have experienced the excitement, if not the trepidation, of standing in the wings before entering onstage. No matter how much we dread what we have to face onstage, there comes a point when we realize we are actually more anxious standing on the sidelines than we are once we plunge into action.

In 'Enter and Exit,' performers in the wings are directed to stand at attention – alert, alive, motionless. Though unseen by the audience, they must consider themselves fully in the dance, as creatively involved as the dancers onstage. The uncertainty of their roles – should they enter, should they not? – is what makes their position so much more difficult than that of their 'active' peers.

Their challenge, poised on the edge of the action, is to distinguish between their own fears and desires, and the needs of the dance. While the temptation is to focus on themselves, the question they must answer is not, "What should I do?" but "What does the dance need?"

If they sense the dance needs a specific element, they must be ready to answer that call, whether they want to or not. Then again, no matter how eager they are to dance, if the piece does not need them, they must choose to remain in the wings.

In life practice we face the same choices of entering the action or remaining on the sidelines, as in the case of a professional determining whether to speak up in a meeting, a teacher leading a seminar, a painter deciding if one more stroke is needed, or a parent counseling a child. If we are really honoring ourselves, others, and our context, we will be impelled to ask at each turn, "What does the situation need?"

As we have seen, the process of accessing the improvisational mind is not always easy. But our willingness to approach the small and large decisions of our lives with this mentality is certain to provide us with direction and yield meaning or insight, often deeper than we could have imagined.

JUDGMENT

Value judgments are destructive
to our proper business,
which is curiosity and awareness.

~ John Cage

Gaining critical perspective is an important aspect of every creative endeavor, if not every human experience. If handled judiciously, such perspective will greatly enhance the creative process and product. If handled unwisely, it can be a destructive force.

Critical perspective is vital for three reasons: it can clarify our own thought to ourselves; it can expand our thought beyond our habitual predilections; and it can help make our work more accessible to others.

Learning how others respond to our actions, gives us information about our impact on the outside world. If we are interested in effective communication, knowing how others perceive what we do allows us to make more considered choices.

As valuable as it is, viewing our creative work or our personal conduct through the eyes of another can also be hazardous. If we become overwhelmed by the judgments of an observer, whether positive or negative, we may lose our own sense of creative confidence or personal integrity.

CREATOR AND CRITIC

The course of a river
is almost always disapproved of
by its source.

~ Jean Cocteau

We all have within us a 'creator' and a 'critic.' The creator is that inner voice which loves to play, experiment, and explore unhindered and unchecked. This voice is counter-balanced by the voice of our critic, providing discipline, perspective, and often an invaluable reality check.

The first lesson we had to learn in *Sonomama* was how to uncover and handle fear. The second was how to reconcile the roles of creator and critic.

Chery & Ran: In the early days, we focused almost exclusively on exploring the creator. We just played.

Over time, we became aware that our improvisations often wandered. Sometimes they had us rolling around on the floor without any shape or direction at all. This was enjoyable enough at first, but eventually, it became repetitive and boring, even to us. Our real objective, after all, was larger.

What motivated our investigation was the desire to learn how to think and create on our feet. Beyond that, we wished to share with an audience, as clearly and legibly as possible, all that we encountered.

What was required to accomplish both aims – creativity and communication – we now decided, was the voice of the critic. So from that point on, even in practice sessions, at least one company member always assumed the role of outside observer. In this way, the presence and perspective of an audience became part of the dance, part of the larger environment to which we listened.

'BAD DANCES'

*Only those who risk going too far
can possibly find out
how far they can go.*

~ T. S. Eliot

There are two sides to every coin. Just as we were congratulating ourselves on having discovered the boon of an audience, we discovered its bane.

Chery & Ran: *Directly after one of our early concerts, our improvisations myste-riously began to go flat. After considerable debate, we speculated that our empha-sis on audience perspective and critical judgment had finally exceeded our creative energies and was now beginning to eclipse them.*

We had over-compensated for our earlier ingenuousness. The critic in our minds had at some point surpassed the creator. And this intense spotlight of self-con-sciousness had dried up the springs of our creativity.

As necessary as it was to develop critical self-discipline, we now saw that the greater imperative was to protect our creativity. We had to find a way to restore our creative courage. We concluded that no matter how finely developed our criti-cal awareness became, the creator must always be master, and the critic, servant.

To diminish our focus on criticism and restore our creative edge, someone came up with the idea of doing 'Bad Dances' – on purpose. The aim of 'Bad Dances' was to break the rules. We encouraged each other to take risks, to enter the absurd, to move without concern for the reaction of audience members or even one another. Our intention was to unearth new material by entering forbidden territory.

In and of themselves, these dances were awful. They were artless, even laughable. They were also indispensable. In a sense, they brought us back to our point of origin. They allowed us periods of temporary regression to tap, uninhibited, our creative sources. And subsequently, we began to think of criticism-free work as an essential part of our on-going creative cycle.

'Bad Dances' worked. They broke new ground. And we were compelled of necessity to revisit them after every performance, when our audience sen-sitivity and critical self-consciousness were at their height. 'Bad Dances' always returned us to the headsprings of our creativity, rescuing us for another round of new explorations.

Real life examples of creative processes akin to 'Bad Dances' are brain-storming, free-associating, and 'blue-skying' – or just plain old play. The purpose in all these approaches is to jumpstart the expansion of thought beyond the habitual into new and uncharted territory, to encourage wide-open thought and imagination where only self-censorship is censored. No attention is given to questions of practicality, policy, or precedence. The wilder the idea, the better.

Chery: My mother, a gifted artist, was often called upon to teach. In her art classes for beginners, students were given at their first meetings nothing but brown wrapping paper on which to draw. The idea, Mom explained, was to treat early sketches as throwaways. None of these drawings were saved.

Her approach encouraged students to explore the process of drawing, rather than fixate on its product. Later, when given standard sketching paper, these students proved far more prepared than most beginners to dive into the creative process, free from crippling self-censorship.

The whole trick to reconciling the creator and the critic, we discovered, is to govern the degree of influence the latter wields over the former. If we begin with the cultivation of the creator, we can gradually and safely develop the critic. But we must never allow the influence of criticism – internal or external – to overwhelm our creative voice.

AUDIENCE ANXIETY

Even if you fall on your face,
you're still moving forward.

~ R. Gallager

Not surprisingly, as in our own beginnings with *Sonomama*, many participants in our *Creative Listening* workshops come hoping to enjoy a few days of carefree exploration and reflection, free from critical self-judgment and the judgment of others.

These participants are not always happy to discover they will be performing in front of an audience, even one comprised only of fellow group members. They are wary on hearing that, following every improvisation, there will be audience feedback coming their way.

For many, the expectation, let alone experience, of judgment generates fear, which in turn impedes their ability to listen and create. All of us have experienced judgment-induced shutdowns at one time or another; and we have all longed at times for judgment-free zones.

Nonetheless, the fact remains that, in reality, we are never without an audience, even if that audience is just ourselves. For this reason, to be creative we must learn how to listen *in spite of* possible criticism with its consequent pull towards self-consciousness.

INWARD AND OUTWARD LISTENING

The more forthright I become in my statements,
the more I learn
from the reactions of others.

~ Alice Miller

Still, some of our participants ask, what is so essential about audience feedback? If what I am doing feels good to me, what's wrong with that?

We say, nothing! It is vital that we begin by listening to our own inner voices and do so with suspended judgment. For this reason, we introduce judgment-free structures into each workshop to ease participants into the audience feedback phase.

For some people, attaining a quality of authenticity through listening without self-censorship may be as far as they are interested in going. For others, listening inwardly is only a *first step* toward achieving the larger goal of more effective, creative communication.

If our larger goal is communication not only with ourselves, but also with others, then audience feedback is an important *second step*. What we have to learn is how to take this second step, to interface with the world, without losing our own creative integrity.

Therapy and Art

What is healing
but a shift in perspective.

~ Mark Doty

Art is, of course, artifice. But as Pablo Picasso said, it is "a lie that tells the truth". We believe art is in some sense a search for 'truth,' for meaning, transformation, and healing. So is therapy. Where then is the line of demarcation between these two?

Daytime television notwithstanding, therapy does not naturally seek a stage but, to the contrary, assumes total confidentiality. Although, like art, a therapeutic experience may entail creativity, its primary purpose is not to communicate with an audience. Because its focus is on the client's experience, not that of an observer, therapy in a theater setting will most likely appear self-indulgent and be of little interest to others.

In comparison to therapy, art is concerned more with the interface of its object with an audience – and therefore, with outward appearance, projection, legibility. It is not, however, therapy's opposite. In fact, even when we turn to art as recreation, we often experience a healing effect.

This effect may occur, in part, because engaging in an art form introduces us to new ways of seeing things. It shifts us into a different way of thinking than we experience in our work-a-day worlds. And art not only allows for self-reflection and expression, but offers new perspectives of the world as well.

Although more concerned with outer appearance than is therapy, true artistic expression is not just decorative or all about show. In *Letters to a Young Poet*, Rainer Maria Rilke talks of art as springing "from necessity."[1] Artists do not usually give their lives to art as a superficial pursuit. They create because somewhere within they are deeply compelled to do so.

---

1   Rainer Maria Rilke, **Letters to a Young Poet**, translated by M. D. Hertner, New York: W. W. Norton and Company, Inc., 1934, 1962.

We could call this pursuit 'therapeutic.' But technically speaking, what makes art *art* rather than therapy is a matter of attention and intention. Art (good or bad) results when the attention of the performer is given both to inner and outer realities, *and* when the intention includes communicating with an audience, even if that audience is the artist alone.

REACTING TO AN AUDIENCE

A storyteller is the person
who creates the atmosphere
in which wisdom reveals itself.

~ Barry Lopez

From the responses of an audience, we gain insight into how and what we communicate to others. Like most of us in real life, improvisers very often have only a vague idea of what others read into their actions. Sometimes the story an observer sees in a particular improvisation will completely blindside the performer.

Chery & Ran: After an improvisational duet between two women, several viewers related a similar account of what they had seen in the dance, a story of a mother and a child. During this feedback, tears came to the eyes of one of the two performers.

Though unaware of this narrative while improvising, the dancer now recognized its similarity to an episode in her early childhood, an incident she had not thought of for many years. On reflection, she acknowledged that, for a lifetime, she had been unconsciously acting out variations of this episode in her day-to-day life.

In this case – and in improvisation, cases like these are not uncommon – the effect of spectator feedback was to help the dancer gain an appreciation for the deep, personal relevance of a dance she herself had created.

Sometimes, audience feedback can leave us feeling overwhelmed, particularly if our performance was deeply and sincerely generated. If the feedback is positive, we may feel profoundly supported. If negative, our very survival may seem at stake, and we may be tempted to become defensive and fight back. Then again, the reflections of an audience may strike us as neither positive or negative, but simply revealing of something unanticipated, as in the story above.

The following are suggestions we offer workshop participants about listening and responding to any spectator feedback, especially if it is critical or in some way difficult to hear:

1. If you feel yourself responding defensively, slow down, breathe, focus, and simply listen to what is being said. As in the practice of the martial art, *Aikido*, rather than confronting your critic with head-on resistance, flow with anything that feels like an attack. Instead of over-reacting, try paraphrasing aloud what you have heard, then checking with your critic for understanding and accuracy. Remember that what we resist persists.

2. Treat criticism as a gift from which to learn. Assume that even a sharp critic has your best interest at heart. And even if he or she does not, you can still use the information advantageously. Look for the nugget of truth, no matter how negative the comments may seem. Note whether you have heard these comments before. You are looking for patterns in your behavior, not one-time occurrences.

3. Work to turn critical judgments into behavioral feedback. If you do not understand the connection between the criticism and your actions, ask your critic for clarification about what specific behavior elicited his or her response.

4. If a criticism continues to appear only minimally connected to your own actions or conduct, treat it as revealing more about the critic than about you. Never take this kind of criticism personally. Instead, look empathically below the critic's waterline for what is driving his or her reactions. How does the criticism make sense in the light of what you know about your critic?

5. You cannot control the responses of others, only your own. If through audience feedback you discover that the effect of your conduct was not what you intended, you now have the opportunity to speak up, clarify your intent, correct the misperception, and make different behavioral choices in the future ... or not.

6. Finally, to gain perspective, distance yourself as you listen to your critic by imagining that you are watching a scary movie from which you will emerge alive and well as you always do. Or picture how significant the criticism you received would seem if remembered a hundred years from now, or if viewed from the moon.

Feedback is essential to realizing the effects of our own behavior. It is indispensable to the success of our interactions with others. In a performance, audience feedback is what helps us understand, from the onlooker's point of view, what about our presentation did and did not work. Without the benefit of such feedback, we may be the last to know.

WHAT DOES NOT WORK

Do not become your own connoisseur.
Sell yourself nothing.

~ Pablo Picasso

The creativity of improvisation is not accessed through rendering, but through surrendering.

As a rule, we have found that an improvisation will be compromised if a performer stops listening and instead makes a conscious, intellectual decision to alter course. This usually occurs when the performer panics – when he or she loses touch with what is happening and is suddenly at a loss for what to do next. It is at this point that an improviser is tempted to make something up.

Reflecting back on an improvisation, an audience can often identify the precise moment when the performance ceased to ring true. At such a moment, the piece suddenly appears flat or contrived, and the audience feels manipulated, grows uncomfortable, or just loses interest.

Usually, observers will be able to describe with some specificity what was happening onstage when the performers 'lost it.' Feedback to this effect helps performers recall what was going on in their minds at that moment, and how and why they lost their confidence, ceased listening, and tried to force the dance.

What Does Work

The moment one definitely commits oneself,
then Providence moves too.

~ J. W. von Goethe

Generally speaking, an audience will say an improvisation 'worked' when they found the piece interesting to watch, or when it provided them aesthetic satisfaction.

Of course, 'aesthetic satisfaction' is highly subjective, varying widely from piece to piece, person to person. We may derive satisfaction from a dance if it displays intriguing or pleasing form, or if it engages us with structural elements, such as reiteration, variation, contrast, and so on. Or we may simply see in the dance a coherent progression and a formal integrity, as if its structure were 'of a whole.'

On the other hand, our satisfaction with a piece may arise purely from the performers' whole-hearted concentration upon the unfolding present, nothing more. Such attention is the heart of successful improvisation. Even if the performer is devoid of any other skill, this attention results in authentic exploration and discovery that is *always* compelling to watch. In fact, without it, all other performance skills are only smoke and mirrors – possibly clever, even technically flawless, but not the genuine article.

When performers are truly listening, there is frequently a convergence of action – a rhythm, direction in space, or movement idea – that two or more performers take up simultaneously. Usually, the performers themselves do not see this moment coming. But suddenly, what the audience is viewing 'comes together' and 'makes sense.'

Even more dramatically, two or more performers who cannot see each other may perform the exact same movement at the exact same time. This coincidence is breathtaking and more common than someone unused to observing improvisation might suppose.

Most profoundly, an improvisation works for an audience when it connects metaphorically with their personal concerns, narratives, and experiences. Here a performance piece can shed light on a viewer's life through his or her own act of interpretation or imagination.

A dance improvisation is about meaning and communication. Whether it works or not is ultimately a question of how well the performers have listened to self, other, and environment, not whether the creative product is judged right or wrong according to some abstract aesthetic standard.

Creative Responsibility

A common phrase among poets is,
"It came to me."

~ Amy Lowell

The audience is part of the environment of any improvisation performance. Learning as improvisers how to take the perspective of critic and creator simultaneously is one of the things we mean by 'listening to the environment.' It is taking into account, or listening to, the audience's point of view.

How can we be watchful and discerning in this role, without becoming overly self-conscious or destructively judgmental of our own actions? How can we protect our own creative impulse?

First, we can allow ourselves to observe, without mental comment, any assumptions or judgments we hear arising in our thoughts. We will then be in a position to recognize, identify, and pass through them. But if we hold onto either assumptions or judgments, they will stop our listening.

Second, instead of asking, "What do I do next?" we can ask, "What does the dance itself need?" Then, all we do is listen. We do not make anything up. We simply trust the appropriate action (or non-action) to surface.

This raises the question, "What is our responsibility as performers to the compositional integrity of the piece as a whole?" The answer may be startling. Our single responsibility is to *be aware* of the compositional elements at work in what is going on around us. We can then rest assured that, if we continue to listen, the appropriate action will become apparent, not only to us, but also to others.

This counter-intuitive approach succeeds as effectively in a corporate boardroom as it does on a stage. It only takes a little imagination to draw the parallels.

Imagine a situation in which all the participants have become hopelessly muddled and entangled – metaphorically or literally. Clarity is lost; the interaction is going nowhere. As simple as it sounds, our one and only job in this circumstance is to *recognize* that the situation has become confused or deadlocked and needs clarification – then listen.

In a dance, this recognition may suggest that, instead of wallowing around on the floor, the performers assume different levels in space, so what each is doing becomes more visible to the audience. In a boardroom, it may suggest slowing down the conversation, allowing time for every individual in the room to be heard.

In either case, it is not our responsibility to rectify the situation all by ourselves. If we do attempt to handle it this way, we will run the risk of having our actions appear contrived or willful and more importantly, we will lose our listening state.

If, on the other hand, we simply focus our awareness on what the situation needs, then pay receptive attention, we can expect appropriate adjustments to occur – in a dance, usually within a few moments. This may be accomplished via our own actions or, sometimes quite surprisingly, the actions of others.

The vital point is this: if we listen, the solution will appear. It is listening, not forcing our own way, that does the work.

SPEECH AND SILENCE

... one of the secrets of this job:
I try not to tell people anything
I really want to tell them.

~ Cheri Huber

Of course, sometimes listening is not so easy. Playing our optimal role in a discussion, performance, or group project may require either restraint to remain silent or courage to speak up. In addition, intuiting the right timing of an action is always essential to success.

Ran: For over fifteen years, I served as one of the trainers for the Interpersonal Communications Workshop (ICW). Originally developed within General Electric by Walter Storey, ICW was a highly structured, five-day workshop with one trainer for every two teams of participants.

When the teams were in session, the trainer's job was to alternate between each team's breakout room, monitoring their progress.

After a year or two, I began to notice that virtually every time I entered a breakout room, the conversation abruptly shifted and lost focus. My appearances seemed to interrupt the flow of conversation.

I fretted about this for some time. I had never believed, even in my university teaching days, that one educates adults by policing them. Such an approach fos-

ters either dependency on, or resentment of, the instructor and a passive attitude towards the work.

I finally raised my concerns with a co-trainer. I proposed we provide each team with clear but minimal directives, and then exit the breakout rooms, letting the teams work out their own solutions, undisturbed.

At first, my colleague was horrified. He was sure the teams would goof off and get nothing accomplished. With fear and trembling, however, he eventually agreed to my plan. The next day, we sat quietly together in the hall outside the four breakout rooms, and trusted the improvisation to unfold.

The effect was electrifying. Not only did the participants seem more energized, but their problem-solving and leadership skills markedly improved, skills they would have occasion to apply immediately, upon returning home to their jobs.

As a result of this structural change, another opportunity materialized. During coffee breaks, when participants emerged from their breakout rooms, I casually engaged individuals in conversation over how things were going.

Very quickly, I discovered that many of these informal conversations were memorable learning events for participants, so much so that I began to offer individual coaching sessions in the evenings. Soon all participants were signing up for these one-on-one conversations.

Now the contact hours between trainer and participant, formerly spent in the breakout rooms, were being committed more profitably and with finer focus to addressing individual needs.

There was, however, one glitch worth noting. At a later workshop, which I happened to be leading alone, I was struck with how silly it seemed just to sit in the hall for hours doing nothing. So the next day, against my better intuitive sense, I brought along a book to read.

Inexplicably, team productivity in this workshop significantly dropped. The structure of the workshop was exactly the same as before, but somehow, I felt less con-

nected, less mentally alert. When participants came out on their coffee breaks, the compelling dialogues, so effective in earlier workshops, did not ensue.

It was then, upon reflection, that I realized what my role during breakout sessions really was: to listen, as if through the walls, as I sat in the hallway alone. Only by staying focused, considering each individual one by one, was I able to discern and address in our private and public interchanges what he or she really wanted.

BEYOND 'JUDGMENTALNESS'

It is one thing to show a man he is in error,
and another to put him in possession of the truth.

~ John Locke

By definition, the creator's role involves a responsibility to promote and protect the creative enterprise. But what is the responsibility of the spectators in this regard? How can they express judgments about what works and does not work without intimidating performers, making them fearful and less able to listen and create?

In order to build mutual trust between performer and observer in our workshops, we encourage participants to reflect on the following questions before offering performance feedback:

1. What was communicated to you in the improvisation? What narratives, if any, did you observe?

2. How clear was the communication of the performers with one another? How legible was the piece as a whole?

3. Did you experience a sense of 'necessity' in the dancers? Did the piece come alive for you? Was there any point at which the improvisation seemed to die?

4. Was there any moment when the dancers appeared to lose it and ceased to listen? What do you think precipitated this disconnect?

5. Was the improvisation relevant to your own life? If so, how?

6. In what ways did the improvisation work or not work for you? What criteria were you using to make this judgment?

7. How do the criteria you applied to evaluate the improvisation compare with the criteria you apply in your own life practice?

8. Finally, as a double-check, is what you are about to say for the sake of the performer, or is it just to make points?

We advise our workshop participants that their immediate task as audience is simply to watch the improvisation unfold. For audience and performers alike, it is important to silence assumptions about what *should* be going on in order to hear and see what *is* going on.

In life as in art, if we are really going to listen, we must initially set aside our judgments of others, if only temporarily, as well as defer the impact of others' judgments upon ourselves until we have heard them out.

Some may question the feasibility or desirability of giving listening a temporal priority over judging. It may seem patronizing or overly solicitous to do so. Our experience, however, is that judgments, made without first listening, often lead to regrettable results – biased, uninformed reactions that are little more than expressions of ignorance, prejudice, or just plain hubris.

The distinction we are making here is between judgment and 'judgmentalness.' The former is a conclusion about what worked and did not work, arrived at only after first listening to the event on its own terms. The latter is a condemnation born of prejudice (pre-judgment), arising from preconceptions and presumptions.

Every performance has a right to be seen on its own terms, fresh and unbiased, not through the lens of preconceived expectations. As soon as we hear judgmental or prejudicial thoughts surface in our minds, we have stopped listening. We are no longer receptive to what is happening, but just biding our time, waiting until it is our turn to speak.

As audience, we will make judgments. But to be supportive of the creative process, we must learn first to suspend our judgments until we have genuinely listened.

CREATIVE TENSION

It takes two
to know one.

~ Gregory Bateson

To summarize, as we discovered early on with *Sonomama's* need for an audience, the skills of critical reflection walk hand in hand with creativity and have an essential role in nurturing the creative endeavor. How these skills are employed, however, is crucial to creative success or failure.

The creatively rich *suspension of judgment,* to which *Sonomama* found it necessary to revert with our periodic regression to 'Bad Dances,' must be balanced by *judgment,* by the critical feedback of an audience. Each represents a necessary element of the creative process. The first is the creator and the second, the critic.

Working together, these two features – judgment and the creative suspension of judgment – generate a tension that keeps the creative flame alive. They allow us to continue both to create and to communicate, to produce new material and to make that material accessible and intelligible to others.

PRESENCE

Wisdom is the reward you get
for a lifetime of listening
when you'd rather have been talking.

~ Aristotle

Listening quiets our fear, frees us from self-consciousness, and awakens us to the present. These three effects of listening provide us with the *presence* necessary for both creativity and effective communication.

Ran: My eldest daughter, Joan, a voice and performance coach, tells of a student with exceptional 'pipes.' Despite prodigious natural talent, [Alessandra's] perfor-mance-fear was so great that in public concerts her voice always emerged disap-pointingly flat and lifeless.

One day in rehearsal, Joan gave Alessandra the assignment to jump up and down as she sang and, at the same time, project her voice to a single point at the far side of the room.

These concrete tasks took all of Alessandra's concentration. Just to breathe was so challenging that her attention shifted entirely away from her self-consciousness and fear. Infused with natural vitality, her voice opened up to display its true beauty and range.

Eventually, Alessandra learned how to perform with this same power and ease while standing still. And if she found herself nervous before a concert, she had only to jump up and down in the wings to relax; then, once onstage, to project her voice to the cheap seats.

Successful communication is dependent in large part on successful perfor-mance, and performance is all about presence. When we undertake any public presentation with an improvisational mind, even a presentation well rehearsed, listening will give us a sense of presence, and the performance itself, an air of freshness and spontaneity.

No Nostalgia, No Regret

A man is rich
in proportion to the number of things
he can let go.

~ Henry David Thoreau

The single most vital component of performing is our focused attention on the here and now. Any performer, artist, or athlete knows the folly of compromising this presence of mind by dwelling on the past.

Clinging to the past, either with nostalgia for a real or imagined good or with regret over some perceived mistake, deflects the performer's attention from the task at hand. Humility and discipline are required to let go of the past. The game, the dance is all.

Chery: From time to time, my mother reminded us of the danger of looking backwards. She recounted the story of an up-and-coming artist whose work was featured in a multi-page spread of an international magazine.

Most people thought this worldwide recognition constituted a tremendous breakthrough for the artist's career. But in fact, at the most crucial level of his work – his creativity – it precipitated just the reverse.

From the time of the article's publication, the artist struggled recapture the humility of his 'beginner's mind.' The glare of early notoriety overwhelmed his every creative effort. The obscurity in which he used to explore new ideas was gone, and he no longer felt the freedom to fail.

PERFORMANCE FEAR

... we're about to take a gander
at the most common obstacles we place in our paths
that stop us from having the confidence
to embrace, practice, and enjoy
the life-stretching experience of improvising.
Here they are: first, there's fear.
And then there's ... fear.
And oh yeah, there's fear.

~ Mark Bergren, Molly Cox,
and Jim Detmar

Occasionally, participants in our workshops question the attention we give to fear. They think of fear as simply one emotion among many. They ask, "Aren't other emotions, such as anger or sorrow, just as important?"

The celebrated pianist and teacher, Georgy Sebok speaks of the inner state of presence in a performer, then echoes what we have discovered about the singular nature and effects of fear on performance and creativity:[1]

> The best technique is one that doesn't exist, a kind of disappearing act, so the real focus needs to be on where the technique comes from: an inner calm, the emptiness from where one can listen. That's not the same as relaxation. You can't play Chopin relaxed. Instead, I talk about fear, and I contrast that with love and hate and other human emotions. Music comes out of those, but it is blocked by fear.

---

1   Thad Carhart, *The Piano Shop on the Left Bank: Discovering a Forgotten Passion in a Paris Atelier*, New York: Random House, 2002.

Confidence and Commitment

It's not what you've got.
It's what you do with what you've got.

~ Mae West

We cannot afford to postpone performing until we have gained perfect confidence in ourselves or mastered fully all we are doing onstage. If we waited for that occurrence, we would all be standing in the wings for the rest of our lives. Much of the confidence we need to perform well comes only with the experience of performance itself.

So, how to perform when we lack confidence? One of the oldest adages in the performing arts is this: regardless of how insecure you feel, *commit* to whatever you do onstage, and it will work. As Ran is fond of saying, "If you wobble, *wobble!*"

But is this nothing more than foolish bravado? Is commitment nothing more than personal willfulness? We believe not, and the difference is a critical one. Commitment, like creativity itself, signals deepened listening and diminished fear.

Willfulness suggests attachment to an outcome, to fulfilling a particular agenda or script. In contrast, commitment connotes open attention, with the intent to embody fully whatever is happening here and now.

The challenge of performing is always to be completely present, one hundred percent invested, in every act. If our intent is only to follow a script, and if insecurity causes us to act hesitantly, we are sure to fail as performers.

In our relationships as well, making the distinction between commitment and willfulness is crucial. Willfulness signals fear, a lack of trust in ourselves or the other. Commitment requires – and builds – trust.

Willfulness urges us to pursue predetermined roles and directions, whether set by ourselves or others. Commitment enables us to stay the course in a relationship by responding to realities as they unfold, attending both the expected and the unexpected with equal openness.

MAKING IT COME ALIVE

I do yoga every day,
but I've never made a habit of it.

~ Krishnamurti

The improvisational mind is present to whatever is happening here and now, no matter how many times these same events may have happened before. It is this presence of mind that allows us to experience all the aspects of our lives with a 'beginner's mind.'

The discipline of performing is the art of experiencing the known as if it were the unknown. Even in improvisation, we can visit familiar territory many times over. Whether performing set scripts or improvisation, success as a performer depends upon our ability to experience what we are doing as if for the first time.

Forms from the past may be usefully revisited, as in the performance of set choreography. But as we have said before, to bring these set forms, or any ritualized event, to life demands the discipline of creative listening.

We have affirmed that listening is an essential skill for lawyers, teachers, ministers, artists, athletes, corporate executives, spouses, parents, anyone who has to think on his or her feet – and communicate. Certainly this is true when seeking new ideas or facing crises. But listening is every bit as valuable when these same individuals are called upon to deliver performances from set scripts or scores.

Chery: When I had taught at Wesleyan only a few years, I had the startling realization that after each of the early classes of a term, I could not recall anything whatsoever about how my students had performed.

I was so concerned with remembering my class plan and so distracted by the practicalities of directing new students in classroom protocol, that it was all I could do to keep my mind one step ahead of the class.

With this recognition of my lack of 'presence,' and with the confidence I eventually gained through the repetition of my lesson plans, I trained myself to step back mentally in the midst of class and pay attention to the present moment. In these instants, improvisation and spontaneity had space to enter.

Giving full attention to how my students were actually receiving the material, I could then flexibly adjust my plans to meet their needs. With the perspective listening afforded, I was also freer to focus on and nurture what I felt was most important – the larger aim and spirit of the course.

Technique and inspiration go hand in hand. By gaining mastery over a script through repeated rehearsals, we as performers are liberated from a preoccupation with the mechanics of the performance. Undistracted by procedure and technicalities, we are freed to embody more vividly the intention of the script.

In general, an audience will pay attention to whatever we as performers attend. If we are focused on our physical technique, it will be difficult for the audience to focus on anything else. If we are fully present (listening) to the image or idea behind the script, the audience, instead of seeing our bodies or personalities, will see the idea.

The confidence that comes with technical mastery, together with the discipline of listening, allows performers to experience in the moment of performance the images and ideas they wish to convey to the audience, and this enables them to communicate these thoughts with greater originality and power.

AUDIENCE

When I listen, they hear.

~ Janice Libby

Communication depends upon the mentality of the audience as well as that of the performer. For the most effective communication, the audience must bring the same presence of mind to a performance as the performer does. If members of an audience, blinded by their own assumptions and prejudices, are not fully present to what is happening, they will be less likely to experience the performer's intent.

Of course, to be 'fully present' is an ideal. In reality, we all travel with assumptions and expectations that inhibit our ability to actually *be* wherever we are.

The degree of presence we as audience are able to achieve depends, in part, upon how aware we are of our assumptions and expectations and their potential impact on our receptivity. Only through this awareness can we distance ourselves *from ourselves* long enough to catch a glimpse of what the speaker or performer is attempting to convey.

Therefore, the more present members of an audience are – *both* to their own assumptions *and* to what is happening in the performance – the more satisfying the interpretative interface between audience and performer is liable to be.

COMMONALITY

Modernist:
If I hadn't seen it,
I never would have believed it.
Postmodernist:
If I hadn't believed it,
I never would have seen it.

~ Anonymous

Each individual will inevitably view and interpret events through the lens of his or her own understanding of reality.

In a proverbial example, two individuals view a glass of water. One sees the glass half-empty, the other half-full. Both, however, end up with the same quantity of water. The actual amount of water constitutes their common reality.

Likewise, performers' interpretations of a dance improvisation may vary widely, depending on the immediate concerns or comprehensive worldviews of the individuals involved. But if each is listening to the present without fear, two dancers with divergent mindsets can harmoniously create and perform together in the same dance.

Here is where being present is so important to collaboration. In an interaction, two individuals, responding to the realities of the immediate present, may recognize the appropriateness or validity of a certain action, even though their construal as to why that action is apt or valid are not the same.

Listening to the 'shared present' has a singular capacity to draw individuals of divergent viewpoints into a common state of mind. And this is what makes creative listening such an invaluable approach to conflict resolution and collective endeavor.

There are many stories told where people from different cultures or social and economic strata are thrust together in crisis situations. Momentarily abandoning years, even centuries of prejudice and alienation, they band together in the face of an external threat to their survival.

In their extremity, attention becomes focused on solving the immediate task before them. They can ill afford to divert precious time or energy to questions of personal blame or condemnation. Any rivalry that surfaces over whose ideas will be adopted must retreat, and any offense taken when a suggestion is rejected is laid aside. The single criterion for their joint action has got to be 'what works.'

Suddenly and unexpectedly, appreciation and respect are born, overcoming ignorance and prejudice. Fears that may have caused division from time immemorial are suspended, replaced by the fresh evidence of first-hand experience.

In such cases, of course, the 'enemy' is perceived as an *external* challenge that all parties face together. If, on the other hand, the enemy is seen as an *internal* challenge, a conflict between parties in one group, the present is still their common ground, and listening is still the road to resolution.

With listening, attention gradually shifts from fear to receptivity. By letting go of defensiveness and abandoning any ambition to defeat 'the other,' all parties can focus on identifying what separates them. This is a first step towards working through their differences.

If this strategy does not work, however, the parties involved can back away from their immediate disagreement and return to (or discover for the first time) what George Lakoff[2] calls their "uncontested core." In a political debate, for example, who would not agree with the core statement, "Democracy is the freedom of a people to govern themselves?"

At this level, there is no contest. The divergence in opinion arises in the particulars, the hows and whys, the refinements that come later. In this refining process, however, the procedure at every impasse is the same.

By returning to the "uncontested core," opponents are able to restart their discussion in a place without fear. Sensitive to one another's hopes and concerns, they can move forward together step by step to address each particular issue as it arises.

Chery: In a discussion on this topic, I asked a friend of mine, a former associate attorney general of the United States, if he could provide me with an example of such a confluence from his experience or historical research. He wrote as follows:

The best example I know is the Constitutional Convention in Philadelphia in 1787. Educated men with wildly different ideas got together behind closed doors

---

2   George Lakoff, *Whose Freedom?: The Battle over America's Most Important Idea*, New York: Farrar, Straus and Giroux, 2006.

and created a new nation unlike any ever found on the face of the earth, answerable to "we the people."

A shared dilemma, if not a shared purpose. The identification of an uncontested core. Above all, earnest and open attention to the present. This is the common platform that listening provides for consensus building and united action in the face of crisis or conflict. The present, like the quantity of water in the glass, provides a common point of departure, and listening without fear opens the way to discover unanticipated concurrence.

Presence has power – the power to communicate, create, even consolidate diversities into dynamic alliance. In seeking peace and accord on any level of our lives, learning to be present is a foundational place to begin.

PART TWO

COMMUNICATING

The universe is made up of stories, not atoms.

~ Muriel Ruckeyser

In our *Introduction*, we stated that our objective in writing this book was to share what we have learned about the impact of listening on two essential aspects of life and work: creativity and communication.

It is our contention that listening, though the humblest of acts, is the foundation of our communication with man, nature, and some would say God, and is the key to every individual's creative participation in making sense of life experience.

Yet we also admitted in the *Introduction* that co-authoring this book in the face of the foundational dissimilarities existing between the two of us has sorely tested, at every turn in the road, the validity of our convictions on the power of listening.

Our dilemma is not just that our concepts of reality diverge. We seem to view and approach *everything* from opposite standpoints. Even our fears are different.

Chery fears disorder and undefined borders. Ran fears too much order and small confines. Ran loves jumping off cliffs to see where he will land. Chery likes a clear sense of direction before she leaps. She unfailingly arrives at her classes with a tested class plan, while he prefers to show up and see what happens.

In our collaborations, Ran is always stepping back to see the big picture, while Chery, heading in the opposite direction, zooms in to pin down the practical realities. To test the validity of anything we say or do together, he seeks to conceive the overall design; she, to fill in the stuff that makes it work. In the broadest sense, Ran's priority is to frame the questions; Chery's, to find the answers.

Of course, we are not alone in having to wrestle such fundamental differences. Humankind has been unable to reach universal agreement on most of the deep questions of existence – the nature of man, the cosmos, or what, if anything, is on the 'other side.' And we, like most of humanity, do not anticipate arriving at a comprehensive religious or philosophical agreement in our work together any time soon. Indeed, that is not our aim.

There is a story reportedly told in India that the earth is supported on the back of a turtle. When the innocent interlocutor asks what supports the turtle, the wise man says, "It's turtles all the way down."

As we can attest from our own collaborations, it does not seem to matter whether we agree that the universe is a pyramid of turtles or not.

What does matter is that we continue to listen to one another with understanding and respect, despite our differing convictions. Seeing the world differently does not prevent us from making inspired improvisations together. In fact, we sometimes astound ourselves by reaching a mutual understanding that *by definition* our most cherished views would appear to preclude.

Recently, after a long, arduous debate on the nature of intimacy, one that yielded just such an accord, Ran exclaimed, "How brilliant of me to bring this question up and get the answer I didn't expect!" We laughed with delight.

Our idea of communication is not to force our neighbor to conform to our point of view, but to keep the conversation going, "all the way down." How is this done? Not by words, but by listening without fear to ourselves – that still, small voice within – and to others.

It takes courage to listen in this way, but in so doing, preconception and prejudice begin to implode and creativity to emerge. Listening to what another person hears, we may catch a new glimpse of self, other, and even a larger R/reality.

PERSPECTIVE

The man who never alters his opinion
is like standing water
and breeds reptiles of the mind.

~ William Blake

If we fail to listen to another's perspective, we are likely to remain bound within the confines of our own conscious and unconscious assumptions. Listening to others allows for variations of experience to enter into our field of vision and to do so as revelatory possibilities rather than occasions for disagreement.

We all have to work out our own meaning, our "own salvation with fear and trembling," as Saint Paul has it. But that need not preclude the possibility of different perspectives.

Of course, listening to stories of another's experience does not necessarily change our own views. But it might. At the very least, having to clarify what you mean and what I mean, may deepen our understanding and undermine the alienating absolutism of rigid adherence to our respective convictions.

THE RISK OF LISTENING

The most dangerous men on earth
are those who are afraid
that they are wimps.

~ James Gillian

It would be hard to underestimate how much we risk when we set aside defended positions and openly listen to another's point of view. This is especially so if our convictions are associated, as they usually are, with a sense of self-preservation.

Ran: A couple of years ago, when my brother, Steve, was Chief of Police at Evergreen State College, he was summoned to intervene in a potentially violent situation. It involved, as he described it, "a very large Afro-American student with a definite anger-management problem."

After police received several calls regarding [Tyrone's] threatening behavior, the college administration had him banned from most public places on campus. He could attend class, but that was it. Nonetheless, his threats of violence and fearsome demeanor continued to elicit numerous complaints.

Responding officers reached the point where they would not approach Tyrone without at least one backup. Any police presence, regardless of their numbers, seemed only to exacerbate the young man's anger. It was almost as if he were seeking public confrontations to provide himself with an audience.

One day, Steve received another distress call. This time Tyrone had been sighted in the campus cafeteria, an area off-limits to him, and everyone there was feeling "very uneasy." When Steve arrived, the dining room was packed, and he was without any backup. He spotted Tyrone sitting on a table, calmly chatting with a fellow student.

Steve approached the trespasser and asked to "have a word." Tyrone's jaw clenched, his eyes narrowed. Steve sat down on the bench attached to the table, purposefully placing himself in what he termed "a vulnerable position, especially if Tyrone decided to get physical."

"You know, you're making some folks around here a bit nervous," Steve began.

The young man smiled, and said quietly, "Yeah, I know."

The ensuing conversation lasted approximately thirty minutes. Most of the time, Steve just listened, asking a question here or there. What he heard was the story of a life spinning out of control.

Tyrone admitted that he was struggling academically, financially, and emotionally. Steve also got the feeling that he was uncomfortable asking for help from anyone, let alone strangers.

When Tyrone finished his story, Steve told him straight up that very few people would be able to cope with such problems and responsibilities. Steve then asked if he could try finding him some help.

There was a palpable sigh of relief as the two men exited the dining hall. On their walk to the office of the Vice President for Student Affairs, where they would begin sorting out available options, the young man confided, "If other people had done what you did, there wouldn't have been any problem. You showed respect. You didn't look at me like I was some kind of rabid dog. You sat down, and we talked. And I could tell that you heard what I said. Thanks, man."

The police department never received another complaint against Tyrone. Two years later, when Steve left the university, Tyrone was still enrolled and experiencing academic success.

ATTENTION

The world is full of obvious things
which nobody by any chance
ever observes.

~ Sherlock Holmes
(Arthur Conan Doyle)

The objectives of art equally involve communication and creativity. This dual concern is one reason why in *Sonomama,* and later in our *Creative Listening* workshops, we found an artistic medium such as dance so effective in exploring and conveying both these themes.

In our early days with *Sonomama,* our interest in creating an artistic product for its own sake was soon overshadowed by the insights we were gaining into the elements of creativity and communication themselves. But ironically, as we turned our concentration away from the artistic product, and focused instead on creative process and communication, we found illuminated *the very essence of art.*

What we discovered was this: first, the inherent capacity of improvisation to foster both creativity and communication comes down to one single element – *attention*; and second, attention is the essence of art.

What differentiates a soup can in an art gallery from a soup can on our kitchen counter? The kind of attention we pay it.

For both artist and audience, the process of making, performing, and observing art is all about paying attention. The frame of a picture or the proscenium arch of a stage says to audience and artist alike, "Attend what goes on within these borders."

Anything *really* attended is transformed – and transforming. The power inherent in attention is art's secret. This power is the means by which art influences individuals, society, and culture in general.

Attention is also the foundation of interpersonal dialogue. When individuals are listened to, they feel respected and valued.

Who among us has not found ourselves at a social gathering, where our companion seems distracted, looking over our shoulder as we try to carry on a conversation. We can barely keep our thoughts together. But if the same companion listens to us with full and interested attention, we may be surprised at how intelligent and coherent, even creative, we become.

Whether we do or do not receive this kind of attention profoundly affects us all. The influence of listening on children is especially apparent.

Children who are never given the respect of undivided attention find it difficult to respect or even to hear their own thoughts. Just one person in a child's experience who will listen quietly, without any agenda but to understand, can and does change – even save – lives.

Chery: *Today the public school system would probably have caught the learning disability early and diagnosed it as dyslexia. But back then, when my sister was in grade school, nobody seemed to know what the problem was or how to address it.*

Kristen recalls a sense of humiliation when asked to present material in front of the class. She failed miserably at spelling bees or when called upon to solve math problems at the blackboard. And as deeply as children do, she would probably have gone on suffering were it not for a very special fifth grade teacher.

Mrs. Short was true to her name. She stood no higher than her students and was as busy as any teacher might be in a lively classroom of fifth graders. But not one student who came under her tutelage fell between the cracks.

Mrs. Short paid attention. She watched every child. She listened to what they said and how they said it, to what they did and how they did it.

What she saw in Kristen was a bright, inventive child who was not learning, one who labored in frustration and despair over any assignment involving writing or math. Then one day, Mrs. Short's attention paid off. She discovered that Kristen loved to dance. And so began her experiment: to teach the whole class in the way Kristen learned best.

On an afternoon soon thereafter, the class was asked to push back their desks. Mrs. Short proceeded to direct them in a movement improvisation exploring the process of photosynthesis. Kristen came home from school that afternoon beaming.

Later, Mrs. Short confided to our grateful parents, "In this creative medium, Kristen stands head and shoulders above everyone else. She is our star." Finally, the class was approaching learning in a way Kristen naturally accessed knowledge. She had been given her own platform on which to perform – and she shone.

In the months that followed, whenever the class approached a topic through creative dance/drama, Kristen caught on right away. For the first time in a classroom setting, she felt validated as a learner. Instead of languishing at the back of the room, she now came forward, engaged. Gradually, her sense of failure and hopelessness reversed.

Kristen went on to graduate from college Phi Beta Kappa/cum laude *and later to develop and teach her own drama/dance approach to education in public and private schools. Science, social studies, language arts, and math – all taught through creative movement. Eventually she wrote a book[1] on her methods, a guide to merging these media into mainstream education.*

Whether the life-crisis facing us is one calling out for better communication or for broader creativity, a little listening can go a long way.

COMPASSION

*The language of friendship is not words
but meanings.*

~ Henry David Thoreau

So far, the stories in this chapter have been instances when listening led someone to say or do something in another's behalf. But there are times when saying and doing are not enough to reach another's need, when listening itself is the highest gift we can give. One of the most profound forms of listening is simple, silent compassion.

Ran: My sister, Marsha, shared with us the following story: "Over thirty years ago, my seven-year-old son, Stephen, came down with what seemed at first only a routine children's ailment. But he did not improve. Eventually, the doctor had him hospitalized.

"Even then I was thinking, 'I know this is serious, but no problem. He's in the hospital, so he'll get better.'" But Stephen did not get better. He experienced a sudden seizure and was placed on life support. The doctors finally determined that the drugs they were prescribing had masked a more serious underlying illness.

"For two days – at least I think it was two days – we were at his side. My mother's heart could not let me believe he wouldn't recover.

"After desperate hours of useless procedures, the doctor pronounced Stephen brain dead. He showed us the results of the brain wave test. Just a straight line. I was

---

1   Kristen Bissinger and Nancy Renfro, *Leap into Learning!: Teaching Curriculum through Creative Dramatics and Dance*, Nancy Renfro Studios, 1990.

finally forced to confront the options. We could continue to keep Stephen's body alive with the machines or let him go.

"We let him go.

"Over the years I have had many opportunities – too many – to listen and comfort other parents who have lost a child. I don't tell them it will get better. I listen, mostly with my heart and spirit. No advice. Just love, hugs, and being there. Sometimes listening is just that."

Beginning from our early years with *Sonomama* through the many years of life practice that followed, we have yet to encounter a situation, no matter how desperate, where listening without fear failed to provide a way.

UNCERTAINTY

... the readiness is all.

~ William Shakespeare

Fronting the uncertainty of the unknown is what made every *Sonomama* performance so scary – and thrilling!

Whenever we went on stage, we never knew which dancers from the company would join us, what parts the musicians and lighters would play, or even what our own roles would be. We had no theme, no plan, nothing but our attention to the present and our willingness to listen. Our only hope was to take things 'just as they were' and be open and ready for whatever arrived.

Improvisation required that we sacrifice the safety and security of the known for the creative possibilities of the unknown. Through experience, we learned, over and again, that fixation on the known undermined our improvisations and stifled our creativity.

EXPECTATIONS

When written in Chinese,
the word 'crisis' is composed of two characters
– One represents danger,
and the other represents opportunity.

~ John F. Kennedy

In *Sonomama*, when we fell back on old scripts and routines, the improvisations invariably failed. If we wanted to cultivate creativity, there was really only one option. We had to let go of expectations and entitlements and listen to the present moment.

Expectations are only phantom realities, which we project into the uncertainty of the unknown. We often think they will prepare us for the future. But fixed expectations can actually hinder the best preparation we have for uncertainty – our ability to respond spontaneously to unexpected realities that confront us.

As evidenced in the immediate responses of officials to the tragedies of 9/11 and hurricane Katrina, crises rarely follow a script. Even with good anticipatory planning, crisis management almost always requires improvisation. When it does, expectations can become our greatest liability.

Neither willful manipulation nor thoughtless assumptions work in improvisation. Be it a crisis situation, a performance, or a relationship, the most dangerous moment is when we stop paying attention to what *is* because we think we know what *should be*, and then try to force the issue. If we make the mistake of assuming we already know what the improvisational situation is all about, we risk missing signs of both its unexpected pitfalls and its possibilities.

Synchronicity, spontaneity, and vivacity go out of our interactions in professional or personal life when one party attempts to manipulate another, or takes for granted what the other will think or do. Any vital working relationship is in spirit an improvisation in the face of the unknown.

It will not do to second-guess the unknown. We must respect it with an almost reverential attention. Only out of uncertainty, watchfully attended, is creativity and renewal born.

LIVING IN THE UNKNOWN

A ship in port is safe,
but that's not what ships are for.

~ Grace Murray Hopper

Many find the unknown frightening and the known a comfortable refuge. At the same time, the unknown is often the very thing that instills our lives with excitement and adventure.

Chery: On a train traveling through Austria, I fell into conversation with a young Swedish man. Troubled by recent news releases documenting the high suicide rates of young people in Scandinavia, I asked my companion if he could shed any light on this alarming trend.

He revealed that, indeed, one of his best friends had taken his own life. My acquaintance went on to say that, though he could not speak for all the others, he knew what had driven his friend, and he gave the following account:

"Because my friend assumed his material needs would be met all of his life by our socialist government, he saw his days stretching before him with no sense of quest, purpose, or adventure. In the face of this specter, he grew depressed, then despondent.

"In his mind, there was no 'unknown.' Without the challenge of an unknown, he felt no real reason to live."

For my companion's friend, the unknown was not intrinsically fearsome, as it is to many. On the contrary, he found it vitalizing, intriguing, essentially life giving.

Although the improvisational mind does pay appropriate attention to the known, like the young man in this sad story, it *thrives* on the wide-open possibilities of the unknown.

KNOWN AND UNKNOWN

Something unknown is doing
we don't know what.

~ Sir Arthur Eddington

What appears to be a blank page is rarely so. We always arrive at a new situation, bearing assumptions from the past. Likewise, no context into which we enter is without its own current and historical suppositions and realities.

The suppositions we are likely to confront in any given situation include our own personal assumptions about life and work, the assumptions and expectations of others, and the cultural assumptions of the environment within which we are operating.

Inherent in any contextual structure, assumptions are ubiquitous. There is no escaping them, real or imagined. Built into the present or borrowed from the past, they are embedded in the context of any new project, and we neglect them at our peril. Given this, what is their role in creativity?

It goes without saying that if we wish to be creative, we must be willing to brave the unknown without falling back into the safety net of the known with its inherited forms. Yet an acknowledgment of the known is also critical to the creative act. It provides our innovative efforts with essential continuity and meaning.

Developing an awareness of the assumptions and realities present in a specific context clarifies the borders within which we are operating, the unspoken elements of the pre-set structure we face. Sensitivity to our context is our preparatory work for creativity and innovation, our first act of listening.

Chery: In his initial days as Chancellor of the University of Alaska at Fairbanks, my father invited faculty and administration to reflect broadly on the educational direction of the institution and to consider structural innovations that might further vitalize the university in its mission.

In a preliminary meeting with one of the Deans, he threw out several models for educational restructuring, some of them radical. His intention was merely to spark interest and get the discussion going. A few days later, Dad was taken aback when the Dean called him, asking when he wanted the memo to go out to faculty, implementing these changes.

Because the university had endured much upheaval over the previous decade – including almost annual presidential turnover – the Dean apparently thought the extremity of Dad's suggestions nothing out of the ordinary and had taken them as an executive order.

My father immediately reconsidered his tactics. What the faculty needed from him at this moment, he realized, was not further change imposed from the top, but a sense of stability and assurance. Now was not the time to assume the mantle of visionary innovator.

Modifying his approach, he sent a memo to faculty and administration asking them to identify "what's working" in each sector of the university. Once areas of strength were determined, he sought to protect and promote them, before introducing any considerations for change.

Gradually, morale rose as faculty and staff saw their efforts recognized, and they gained the confidence to move forward with innovation. Only after carefully considering the known, could the university embark successfully on a creative encounter with the unknown.

Awareness of a pre-existing situation need not limit our creativity. It can, in fact, furnish information necessary to make our work more directly responsive and relevant to other people involved.

The known provides us with a sense of the history, the pre-condition or mental context into which new acts enter and unfold. Knowledge of history alerts us to the relation and relevancy of the past to our present acts. Seen in this way, a conscious awareness of the past enriches the improviser's ability to create meaning.

Once incorporated and digested, any contextual understanding will subconsciously impact our creativity. For the seasoned improviser, knowledge of the past and its present ramifications will usually operate without obtrusively interfering with his or her improvisational mentality. For the beginning improviser, this may not be the case.

Beginners are sometimes influenced overmuch by the script of the past. Imposed structures of any kind tend to direct thought – sometimes toward creativity and sometimes towards habit and mindlessness. It is well to remember that the past, like any pre-set script or structure, can impede listening and creativity unless it functions in a supporting, not a dominating role.

STRUCTURE AND CREATIVITY

The last of human freedoms
is to choose one's attitude
in any given set of circumstances,
to choose one's own way.

~ Viktor Frankl

Any context we enter may exhibit multiple structures inherited from the past. Or a marked absence of them. Either circumstance can prove fertile ground for creativity.

Assumptions, our own or others', delineate structures in which we operate, but they need not prescribe all our thoughts, feelings, and actions within these structures. A willingness to listen and respond afresh to the present moment is the salient factor determining our creative capacities in any situation.

Creative listening, or paying attention without fear, is the improvisational mind's response to the uncertainty of the unknown. The security inherent in the known – in assumptions, pre-set scripts, and agendas – may provide a sense of freedom from fear, but it is not true safety if it does not prepare us to respond creatively to the realities of a changing world.

Ran: From the beginning, creativity was central to my concept of what liberal arts education was all about. My primary concern as a teacher was to engage students in a way that developed their ability to question and think for themselves.

I usually prepared for my courses by rereading the assigned text directly prior to each class meeting. In so doing, I hoped to give students my freshest, sharpest thinking on the topics before us.

On one occasion, however, I arrived not having done my homework. To my surprise, what ensued was one of the most interesting class discussions I had ever witnessed. Some time later, I found myself again unable to reread the text before class, and again the discussion was outstanding.

Was there a pattern here? To test this theory, I purposely arrived to teach the following class without having reread the text, and once more the discussion was a great success.

Upon reflection, I concluded that showing up without a spiel to lay on my students made me more inclined to listen than to speak, to raise questions than to provide answers. Not an easy role when I really felt I had something to say!

But when I spoke less, students seemed encouraged to offer up their own ideas more readily. And if I listened long enough, not only did they anticipate my thoughts, they came up with ideas I had never considered.

This is not to say that diligent research – doing our homework – does not have its necessary role. The issue here is not scholarship (the known) vs. spontaneity (the unknown). Both the certainty of the known and the uncertainty of the unknown play a critical part in fostering creativity.

The essential point is this: what enables us to experience the known and the unknown as equally positive forces, is listening.

IDOLATRY

*Much of the wisdom of one age
is the folly of the next.*

~ Arthur Schopenhauer

One of the most common reactions to fear of the unknown is to hang obstinately onto the familiar. How many times have we heard, "But this is the way we've always done it?" If we are not alert to the fear underlying this resistance to change, repeating old forms can turn into a kind of idolatry.

In the world of dance, set choreography might be viewed as an attempt to cling to the past, to repeat the same improvisation twice. The possibility of repetition usually fosters a sense of security. But even in performing ritual ceremonies, the improvisational mentality is necessary.

Unless transformed by creative listening, choreographic forms of all kinds, as well as social institutions in general, will lose their vitality or relevancy and eventually become obsolete.

Set structures can be useful, even essential for a time, yet though a major motivation behind establishing them is the desire for stability and permanency, the expectation that static forms will remain permanent is a delusion. They never achieve permanency, quite the opposite. When something stops moving, it dies.

Or worse. A structure maintained past its time can effect the antithesis of its original purpose.

Chery: There is a rather funny-sad story I remember reading many years ago.

When plumbing came into common use in small-town America, a crusty old-timer, living on with his grown children in the family home, refused to change his lifelong habits. To the embarrassment of his offspring, he insisted on continuing to use an old outhouse at the back of the property.

His children's pleas that its presence made the family appear backward, that it constituted a health hazard, even that it emitted an offensive odor were obstinately ignored. In all seasons and in all kinds of weather, the old man trudged down a well-worn path to the antiquated structure. And to all entreaties, he parroted the axiom, "It's a dirty bird that fouls its own nest."

What the old man prized as a symbol of cleanliness, his offspring despised as its very reverse.

As patriarch of the family, the old man was begrudgingly given his due, while his children suffered stoically. But when he finally died, the little house in the back of the yard was dismantled within the hour.

Institutions

How can one live with a soul
in an apartment?

~ Marina Tsvetaeva

With all the labor that goes into any new creation, there is a natural desire to perpetuate the original inspiration and further expand its creative possibilities and applications. This usually impels the development of some supporting institutional structure.

Institutionalizing an idea, however, is always risky. The structure that first served to protect the idea may all too easily constrict and eventually crush it.

One of the ways an institution can destroy its instigating impulse is to fail to change with it. To preserve both the idea's and the organization's ongoing vitality, competing needs for stability and growth must be balanced.

To this end, an institutional structure can be designed to evolve along with its originating idea, as does a mollusk with its living shell. Or, following the example of the hermit crab, an outgrown structure can be abandoned for a larger, more expansive one. Either way, the primary concern must remain the ongoing development of the idea itself.

Another way the protective structure of an institution often backfires is by becoming a refuge for employees seeking to promote and preserve their own private interests. How many times have we seen an institution that began with the self-sacrifice of one generation become an occasion for the decadence and dissipation of the next?

In cases like these, the self-interest that sets in will not necessarily destroy the institution, but it will darken and eventually eclipse the development of its originating idea or vision, even to the point, as we have said before, of actually reversing that idea and perpetuating its opposite.

If, however, the interests of the organization remain uppermost in the minds of its members, the focus of day-to-day operations are less likely to be deflected. Policies will keep pace with the growth and evolution of the founding idea and its purpose.

Institutions themselves need creativity to survive. Their inherent emphasis on continuity and stability works against change, but to keep pace with a changing world, any institution, like a phoenix, will eventually need to reinvent itself in order to sustain its vitality.

Ran: At the time I began consulting with General Electric in the early '80s, the newly appointed C.E.O., Jack Welch, was in the process of turning the company, and the entire corporate world, upside down.

First of all, Welch determined to sell any GE company that wasn't ranked #1 or #2 in its area of business. Three-generation GE families were reeling, as were new-comers who had anticipated a secure and uninterrupted career.

To make matters worse, Welch declared that company loyalty to employees and employee loyalty to the company were a thing of the past. From now on, return to the investors was all that mattered.

Needless to say, in the face of such titanic organizational and cultural change, employee anxiety was high and morale at a rock-bottom low. Participants arrived at the Interpersonal Communications Workshops (ICW) I led wondering if they would have a job by the end of the week. Their fears surfaced mostly as anger, sometimes depression.

Older managers complained that the rules of the game had changed. Traditional, authoritarian managers were no longer tolerated. They now had to have 'touchy-feely people skills.' Communications workshops were labeled 'charm school.' They were often seen as punishment, or even worse, a prelude to dismissal.

I spent many hours late into the night listening to the heartache. Many seemed like lost children, abandoned by fickle parents to the whims of fate. While some threw temper tantrums, others considered what it would be like to be 'adults' in this new world.

Gradually, I began to hear strategies for surviving – even succeeding – within the new GE. In addition, stories surfaced of basement entrepreneurs starting their own businesses in the hopes of eventual independence.

The employees who survived were those who found the courage to move into the unknown, whether as reinvigorated members of the corporation or fledgling entrepreneurs. Within GE, team loyalty replaced company loyalty. As GE became a corporate trendsetter, a new sense of pride began to emerge.

Like a river flowing within its banks, the lively vitality of improvisational thought has a transformative effect on institutional stability. In the short run, it will renew and perpetuate the life within and around any set form it inhabits. Eventually this same mentality will, by degrees, transform that form. And in the long run, it is, perhaps paradoxically, the improvisational mentality itself, not the set structure, that will predominate and endure.

MANAGERS

I am a man of fixed and unbending principles,
the first of which is to be flexible at all times.

~ Everett Dirksen

Managers are usually thought of as overseers whose job it is to maintain the order and continuity of the institutional structure. But enlightened administration requires, even demands, creativity and listening. Listening can become the source of institutional stability and mobility, of equilibrium and innovation alike.

Chery: *When Dad first accepted the position of Chancellor at the U of A, he was warned of considerable student unrest on campus. Determined to meet this issue head on, he set up a weekly forum in the Student Union Building, where students were invited on Thursday afternoons to meet with him publicly and voice issues of concern.*

At first, these meetings were packed, but after several weeks, they dwindled in size. Exchanges between students and administration calmed, as students began to feel their concerns were heard by the powers that be.

To this same end, Dad made a point of showing up at a wide range of campus events. On any given night, he and my mother might drop in for the first half-hour of a lecture by a visiting physicist, then catch the second act of a student play, and end up at the last quarter of a basketball game.

Students and faculty alike eventually came to view this new administration as accessible, one that witnessed their trials and triumphs, shared in their concerns, and engaged them in respectful dialogue.

Survival within an institution can be a daily challenge, but it can also be an opportunity for real creativity and service. The bureaucratic needs of institutional life, just as much as research and development, require the ingenuity of improvisation and creative listening, both to promote the stability of the institution and to serve its evolving mission.

FOUNDERS AND ENTREPRENEURS

Behold the turtle.
He makes progress only
when he sticks his neck out.

~ James B. Conant

Entrepreneurs or founders in general are by nature improvisers *par excellence*. Given this leaning, they often come into conflict with the stabilizing elements required of institutional life. The classic dilemma an entrepreneur experiences is the tension between innovation and preservation, between 'improvisation' and 'choreography.'

The more successful innovators become, the more difficult it is for them to continue operating improvisationally. As a founder's enterprise develops, organizational structures are needed to support its expansion. Once the business outgrows the possibility of face-to-face interaction, procedures are required to provide operational consistency and order.

At this point, unless the entrepreneur hires a manager to oversee the company, the company will often flounder. In the corporate world, the manager's role is to develop institutional structures – flow charts, hierarchies of command, rules, and regulations – necessary to facilitate production and marketing, a role in which the founder is rarely interested.

As improvisers and innovators, entrepreneurs are seldom comfortable with a choreographed script. Because they value creativity more than the production of a standardized product, they feel frustrated by procedures that inhibit their creative bent, procedures everyone else in the organization is now expected to follow.

As a result, the entrepreneur may gain a reputation as a wild card, often leaving colleagues uncertain what will happen next. Employees may even regard the company's founder as a saboteur of his or her own creation. If this occurs, the founder risks being viewed by associates as a liability to the company, and, in the extreme, ending up in mortal combat with the Board of Directors.

Founders can successfully survive such conflicts, and even continue on in their companies, if they build into company culture an overriding commitment to creativity, or if they position themselves as head of development and let others manage day-to-day operations.

As a last resort, a more radical alternative exists for the entrepreneur, but one that in some cases may prove the most workable. It is simply to relinquish the ownership of the company, once it is up and running, and launch a whole new enterprise.

Chery & Ran: In our ventures with Listening Unlimited, *the two of us have experienced perpetual creative tension between innovation on the one hand and preservation on the other – the entrepreneur and the manager.*

When we balance these two roles successfully, our projects leap forward. When fear pushes us too far in one direction or the other, action is stymied.

One day, in discussing an important aspect of this book, we had a particularly try-ing session, where once again the struggle between the entrepreneur in one of us and the manager in the other threatened our progress. We were left uncertain how to move beyond this impasse, but it was clear that if no solution were found, the book would never make it to publication.

We each took some quiet time on our own to listen. Eventually, we agreed on a course of action that was not the first choice of either, but at least minimally acceptable to us both.

Later, in recounting to one another the thought processes we had followed to come to our individual decisions, we discovered with no little surprise that each assumed he or she was the one who had made the sacrifice and given in.

But there was another small detail to this story, a revelation that totally aston-ished us. In speaking with our respective confidants that very day, we had both expressly likened our own actions to those of the harlot who came before King Solomon, seeking the return of her child.

As Bible readers will recall, two harlots, living alone together in a house, gave birth within three days of one another. One woman inadvertently overlaid her child in the night. Awaking to find it dead, she switched the infants while the other woman slept, taking the live child to her own bed and placing the dead baby in the arms of her friend.

The two women came before King Solomon: the wronged mother seeking justice and the return of her child, the other protesting her innocence. With no witnesses save these two, Solomon asked for his sword. The account continues[1]:

> *Then he said, "Cut the living baby in two – give half to one and half to the other."*

---

1   I Kings 3: 25-27, The Message: The Bible in Contemporary Language, translated by Eugene H. Peterson.

The real mother of the living baby was overcome with emotion for her son and said, "Oh no, master! Give her the whole baby alive; don't kill him!"

But the other one said, "If I can't have him, you can't have him – cut away!"

The king gave the decision: "Give the living baby to the first woman. Nobody is going to kill this baby. She is the real mother."

In our own far less dramatic case, knowing the 'child' was lost if a way could not be made to move the book project forward, and seeing no other alternative, we each gave in to save it. Only then did we discover that, to a depth we had not imagined, we had been 'of one mind' all along.

Laying aside deep concerns and cherished desires, we listened to the situation present before us. And different as we were in our tolerance of risk versus structure, we found a single door we could pass though together.

An interesting postscript: though at the time we considered the choice we made a compromise, something we rarely make together, it proved in retrospect to be among our finest decisions.

Different individuals have different levels of tolerance for certainty and uncertainty, the known and the unknown. But no matter where we find ourselves on this spectrum, our creative productivity is determined principally by one thing – our open and receptive attention to the present.

In any role, the crucial question for each of us to continue to ask is, "Am I listening?"

MEMORY

All human beings should try
to learn before they die
what they are running from
and to, and why.

~ James Thurber

Because memory plays such a significant role in how we register what is going on within us and around us, its impact on our creative voice deserves consideration.

At first glance, creativity would appear to favor the new over the old, invention over memory, with its sense of continuity with things past. From this perspective, it would be reasonable to conclude that memory itself, not just fear, is an impediment to creativity. But actually, depending upon our attitude toward it, memory can work as readily for creativity as against it.

If memories are of positive experiences, or of difficult ones through which we have gleaned valued lessons, they will tend to strengthen our trust, faith, and confidence, and thereby enhance our ability to listen. If, on the other hand, memories are fearful or seductive, they may arrest our thought processes, closing down our receptivity to the new.

Whether the effect is positive or negative, the role of memory as a present, active influence in consciousness must be understood in order to exploit our full creative potential.

Confidence and Courage

Better hazard once than always be in fear.

~ Thomas Fuller

Some memories build confidence born simply of the known. Repeating old behaviors with their reassuringly predictable outcome supports our efforts to enter the uncertain present while keeping our fear of the unknown at bay. Rehearsals build assurance.

Similarly helpful is a familiarity with 'the lay of the land' that remembered experience can provide. The recognition of familiar territory stabilizes us by providing a sense of perspective and orientation.

Of course, neither repetition nor recognition is creative in and of itself. But what we remember of previous experiences where our efforts met with success can give us greater courage to face endeavors that do require creativity.

Overwhelming Memories

One need not be a chamber to be haunted;
One need not be a house;
The brain has corridors surpassing
Material place.

~ Emily Dickinson

Instead of gaining confidence with experience, there are times when we may feel overwhelmed by the remembered past. Any preoccupation with the past – positive or negative – is antithetical to innovation. It impedes our ability to listen and, thereby, to create something new.

On one hand, our positive memories may be so seductive that we rehearse them *ad nauseam*, seeking to recapture and relive our glory days. As a result, we may become stuck in the past, like tearful brides re-running their wedding videos day after day.

Fearful memories can be equally distracting. Once bitten by a dog, we may find ourselves incapacitated in the face of all dogs, no matter how benign.

Even more debilitating are memories so traumatic they are lost to consciousness altogether. Such 'unremembered' memories can impel us blindly to repeat behaviors even we ourselves do not understand.

In all of these instances, the question is the same. How do we maintain, even enhance, our ability to create the new in the face of the past?

Our approach in improvisation is to observe our memories 'just as they are' and embrace them as powerful beginning points in the creative process. We simply pay attention to them without judgment.

Becoming aware of seductive or fearful mental images, without identifying with them, can transform their impact. Observing them from a distance diminishes their hold over us, and provides us with fresh perspective and insight on their import and impact in our lives.

As we gain both a clearer understanding of our past and an expanded sense of our present possibilities, we are gradually freed from merely rehearsing the past to perceiving and pursuing innovative alternatives. By paying attention to our memories, we uncover their potential as a creative wellspring.

Chery & Ran: At one time, Sonomama *was invited to perform for the patients and staff at a nearby psychiatric hospital. During the performance, we introduced an improvisational structure entitled 'Sculpture Dances.'*

Here, one person in the role of sculptor molds the dancers' bodies into shapes, positions them in relation to one another in space, then joins the audience to see what will happen. The performers, paying close attention to these shapes and spatial configurations, intuitively follow their implications into a dance.

To conclude our performance, we invited members of the audience to use **Sonomama** *dancers to create their own sculptures. One patient, who appeared very depressed, nonetheless volunteered. He proceeded to create a pyramid of danc-*

ers, three side by side on their hands and knees, then two kneeling on the backs of the first trio, forming a second tier, and finally our smallest dancer on top.

At the end of what was for us a very awkward dance, our sculptor seemed oddly relieved, almost jubilant. When we asked him his motivation for placing the dancers as he did, he replied that he just wanted someone else to feel and understand the kind of burden he faced every day of his life.

By setting up this dance, the patient in this story was able to share with others an inner world where he felt engulfed and alone. Then by observing his own creation, he gained distance and some reprieve from the memories, feelings, and images that daily overwhelmed him. In the end, he even witnessed his negative feelings transformed by the dancers into a positive source of creativity.

MEMORY AND MEANING

The past is never dead.
It's not even past.

~ William Faulkner

Pleasure and security are often found in our perception of continuity between the present and the past. When an improvisation ends spontaneously with some subtle variation of its beginnings, we as audience experience a certain satisfaction. Perhaps we relish this juxtaposition of freshness and continuity in the same artistic field, because it is in this concurrence of past and present that we create meaning.

Meaning is made through association, usually in some narrative form.[1] In all societies, cultural values and spiritual teachings are passed down in the form of parables from one generation to the next. This format is successful in part because ideas captured in story or metaphor are easier to grasp

---

1   Even within the non-linear, anti-narrative world of post-modernism, fragmented images are paradoxically held together or brought into association by juxtaposing disparate elements in the same space-time frame or continuum.

than abstract statements of principle or belief. The relationship of one idea to another is easier to see – and to remember.

In improvisation and in life, we regularly live out, consciously or unconsciously, the stories we generate around what has happened in the past, is happening in the present, or is anticipated to happen in the future. This is why becoming cognizant of these mental constructs is so important to the meaning and direction of our lives.

These narratives also sustain our ability to retain memories. We remember past experiences by embedding them in larger narratives, which give place and value to discrete memories, too myriad or insignificant to be retained otherwise.

Of course, our stories are in reality creative acts, never literal transcriptions of actual events. In the process of placing an event within a narrative, we recast what 'actually' happened. We creatively shape, and yes, even distort, what we remember.

Like recorded history, memory is not a reliable testimony of events. And like any historical text, it creates a 'reality' that is at best semi-real.

'Remembered' Memory

Dare to know.

~ Emanuel Kant

For members of the audience, an improvisation may awaken a plethora of memories from individual past experiences, memories which evoke in spectators, associations and meanings entirely unknown to the performers.

In some cases, an improvisation may closely resemble and, in so doing, reinforce past experience. This is an important function of performance; reinforcement is a basic need. The desire to communicate our experience of life, or have our experience confirmed by others, is manifest in all cultures and in countless artistic expressions.

In art, desire for communication and confirmation is shared by both artist and audience. The playwright Eugene O'Neill's haunting depiction of his family in *Long Day's Journey into Night*, a stunningly rendered self-disclosure, is usually considered his finest work. And what spectators have failed to detect aspects of their own families in this play?

Reinforcement is only one side of the coin, however. The other is revelation. In some instances, an improvisation may provide a mirror through which the audience sees confirmed what they already feel or believe. In other cases, the dance and how it unfolds reveal an altogether new way of seeing things.

Chery & Ran: In our workshops, we sometimes present an improvisational structure entitled 'Family Portraits,' a variation on 'Sculpture Dances' mentioned previously. In 'Family Portraits,' one dancer sculpts a group of dancers as if posing them for a family photograph, but without identifying whom each dancer represents in the family group.

At a recent workshop, one sculptor immediately came to tears as the dance he had initiated began to unfold. In contrast, other audience members broke into laughter. Lacking knowledge of the sculptor's associations with struggles his family had recently endured, these spectators were moved by very different associations of their own.

Of course, the dancers themselves had no idea what they were imparting to the sculptor or any other viewer. They were absorbed in listening to their own actions, relationships, and associations within the matrix of the dance.

At times, both 'Sculpture Dances' and 'Family Portraits' confirm the experience of the sculptor, and this can in itself be gratifying. At other times, the improvisation surprises the sculptor with the direction it takes.

In witnessing this particular dance, our sculptor, despite the tears, was inspired by what he saw. He found in the dance's narrative new insight into his family's dynamics and a more hopeful vision for their future.

'UNREMEMBERED' MEMORY

*Those who cannot remember the past
are condemned to repeat it.*

~ George Santayana

We consciously relive memories of joy and sorrow in the present, in what Sören Kierkegaard called "the second enjoyment." But if we are unaware of our 'memories,' the present may be overwhelmed by an 'unremembered' past. When this happens, our ability to create will diminish, and we may end up with some form of creator's block.

As we have seen in our discussion of koans, all of us tend to revert to habitual behaviors when we find ourselves either suddenly at a loss for what to do next or shut down by fear. At such points, we instinctively flip onto automatic pilot. Our bodies take over as our minds close down, 'remembering' what the mind has lost. And when this happens, we revert to the safety of scripts without even realizing it.

Ran: My mother did not find out she was adopted until well into her fifties, after her adoptive mother died. Within a few days of the funeral, it became apparent to Mother that virtually everyone – her cousins, even her boarding school roommates – knew of her adoption. It was the big family secret.

One can only surmise what an incredible effort it must have taken on her part to remain in the dark about something so intimate and yet so widely known among family and friends.

Growing up, I sometimes wondered at the disparity between my mother's lack of curiosity and her native intelligence (which, ironically, she applied in the safety of her late night solitude to the reading of every mystery novel ever written). She never probed the depths of anything, never asked questions of me (thank goodness!) or, to my knowledge, anyone else.

But as I look back I realize, Mother succeeded in avoiding emotional stress in all aspects of her life the same way she avoided the fact of her adoption. It was as if she possessed an intuitive sense that deeper investigation into sensitive matters of any kind might uncover some unbearable truth.

From my subsequent work in improvisation, I came to identify as an unexplored koan the unvarying face she so carefully constructed and presented to the world: her naively optimistic and good-humored mien.

At times, something from our past may seem so frightening that we quarantine it from consciousness altogether. In order to keep such fearsome inroads at bay, of course, we must maintain a constant vigil. Still, inroads are bound to occur subliminally, shaping how we act and react and inhibiting our creative potential.

When we cannot understand why we keep repeating the same deleterious behavior over and over, we will probably, upon investigation, find a ghost lurking in our closet. In such cases, the past, even though 'unknown,' will remain with us until the 'unremembered' memory is uncovered and the meta-narrative that failed to incorporate it is revised or replaced.

When we are aware of our memories, the past is available for creative transformation. When we are unaware, the past can become the tail that wags the dog, and if we do not find a way to interrupt the flow of our behavior and listen for a new beginning, we will find ourselves endlessly acting out the same repetitive patterns.

Chery & Ran: An improvisational structure particularly enjoyable for its element of surprise is entitled 'Cut Piece.' During this improvisation, any dancer may at any time shout, "Cut!" At that point, all dancers in the piece freeze. After listening for a few seconds to their frozen positions, they resume moving, either to continue with the themes of their previous dance or to begin a new dance altogether.

At a recent workshop, following the performance of this structure, one participant in the group, a psychiatrist, spoke up. "It just came to me in a flash," he exclaimed. "This is exactly what my teenage daughter needs."

[Gordon] went on to explain. "We all tend to carry on our lives with some degree of continuity. What we begin, we usually continue doing. When we are in a dance, we tend to stay in that dance, for better or worse.

"But the 'Cut Piece' introduces the idea of a time-out right in the middle of the action. It gives us the chance to take a deep breath and step outside ourselves, if just for a moment.

"This ability," Gordon asserted, "is what my daughter needs to know she has. When she falls into self-defeating patterns which she feels unable to alter or control, she can just say, 'Cut!'"

At a later workshop, Gordon reported that he had, in fact, introduced this concept to his daughter. "You don't have to go along with what is 'prescribed' by your own scripts or those of your peer group," he told her. "Just because you have begun a certain behavior doesn't mean you have to continue in it. To change, all you need to do is stop in your tracks, listen, and then begin again."

With gratitude, Gordon informed us that this idea had seemed to resonate with his daughter who thoughtfully accepted his suggestion.

In improvisation, as in any creative endeavor, one of the primary challenges is learning how to generate new forms or stories from old impulses. Besides 'Cut Pieces,' other improvisation structures such as 'Koans' and 'Counter-Koans' regularly provide graphic examples of this alchemy. But almost any improvisation, no matter what the foundational structure, will in some way serve the process of creative transformation from old to new, if we will just pause and listen.

TRANSFORMING OUR BEGINNINGS

*[Creativity is] a process of catching
the moment of attention
and following it beyond the expected.*

~ Jordan Smith

Generally speaking, fear impels us toward 'fight or flight' and away from listening and creativity. The two men in the following story are an astonishing exception. They chose neither to continue fighting nor to flee in the face of their violent past.

Ran: A few years ago, I met a survivor of the genocide in Burundi who had suffered severe machete wounds. There was a slash across his face, such that when he cried, he said, the tears came out of his nose.

Somehow, he had survived and eventually returned to his small bicycle shop in the rural countryside. After becoming involved in the national campaign for mediated reconciliation between Tutsi and Hutu tribal members, he met face to face with his attacker and, incredible as it seems, ended up hiring him as an employee in his shop.

The two men now work side by side, fixing bicycles and helping restore their ravaged community. Both men refuse to be bound by, or reduced to, their fearful memories. They have been able to transform their genocidal beginnings into an improbable partnership for peace and reconciliation.

No doubt, these countrymen did not forget what they had undergone. And yet, neither did they continue to tragically reenact it. Unlike trauma victims prone to repeat their victimization – whether as reoccurring victims or as victimizers of others – these men followed their memories "beyond the expected" into a new sense of possibility.

None of us needs to remain trapped in the past. By humbly and earnestly listening to ourselves, one another, and the greater physical, social, and spiritual contexts of our lives, we can use our memories – whether positive or negative – as a point of departure into something new, into something liberated, and upon reflection, larger and more meaningful.

As we are not our fears, we are also not our history. What we hold in consciousness now is what we experience ourselves to be. And that can change.

IDLENESS

It is in our idleness, in our dreams,
that the submerged truth
sometimes comes to the top.

~ Virginia Woolf

Throughout our short history as a nation, the 'business' of Americans has been 'busyness.' Unlike a number of our international friends, we pursue even our leisure with the same relentless zeal as we do our vocations.

The business of creativity, however, requires just the opposite of busyness. It actually requires *idleness*. An idle state of mind, we believe, possesses a hidden potential, essential to imagination. Entered into with the improvisational mind, idleness is the very seedbed of creativity.

Creativity is by nature iconoclastic – breaking old forms and making new ones. And in America at least, idleness, far from being a mainstream value, is considered counter-cultural if not downright seditious. A respect for, even celebration of, idleness as a source of creativity is, no doubt, counter-intuitive as well. After all, how can we create something by doing nothing?

What we are contending here is that creativity depends upon listening, and that our ability to listen depends upon a mental state of idleness. We cannot listen optimally with a cluttered mind, or in the clamor of the marketplace.

The Devil's Workshop

... the cost of a thing
is the amount of what I will call life
which is required to be exchanged for it ...

~ Henry David Thoreau

The creative process is much like driving an old stick-shift automobile, where we must pass through 'idle' in order to shift gears. Creativity requires we first disengage – shift into idle and listen without judgment – before we launch into action. But cultural bias discourages this essential intermediary step.

One of Ran's grandmother's favorite sayings was, "Idle hands are the devil's workshop." Ran took this to mean that, if he stayed busy enough, the 'devil' could not lay hold of him. Over the years, he has come to believe that the opposite is also true. The devil abides in our busyness as well.

Traditionally, our elders have feared that idleness leads to dissipation, even self-destruction. But certainly, not to creativity. Indeed, early Church fathers declared 'curiosity' a dangerous sin.

Why is idleness so threatening? Perhaps, we are afraid of the potential 'nothingness' involved, and would rather the hyperness of diversion or the security of old habits and routines. We would prefer working hard at the same-old-same-old to the possibility of a flare-up of imagination.

Unproductive Idleness

If water derives lucidity from stillness,
how much more the faculties of the mind!

~ Chuang Tzu

There exists, of course, uncreative idleness born of self-indulgence or fear – fear of work, fear of failure, even fear of success. The difference between these barren forms of idleness and the rich, fallow idleness from which creativity springs is not always easy to distinguish. But, not surprisingly, our experience indicates that the factor differentiating the one from the other is the presence or absence of listening.

Listening introduces a quality of attention and alertness, a readiness to act when the time and opportunity are right. Self-indulgence and fear lack this underlying vitality. They would have us either sit back passively on our heels or scatter our attention and follow through with nothing.

FEAR OF IDLENESS

All a man's troubles
come from not knowing
how to sit still in one room.

~ Blaise Pascal

For most Americans, all manifestations of idleness are highly suspect, and are usually seen as signs of moral turpitude. To be idle is to be irresponsible.

Besides its implication of moral failure, idleness can be frightening. In its open, 'empty' spaces, we are inescapably confronted with ourselves. When busy, we have little time to reflect on the big questions of life, such as our greater purpose or ultimate worth.

A state of idleness can resemble the profound emptiness of those returning from war, or those who have lost a job, experienced a divorce, or faced an empty nest.

Entering into a state of idleness is often associated with entering literally into a 'wild' space – a garden, woods, or wilderness – the space where the subconscious comes alive. Characters in Shakespeare's plays enter a forest to come out transformed. Religious figures retreat into the wilderness to hear the voice of God.

Ran: *[Daniela], a Fortune 500 company executive, was attending one of my communication skills workshops. In a private conversation late one evening, she told me the following story:*

"I have a reputation in the company as a troubleshooter. Whenever one of the company's plants is in trouble, they send me in to fix it. In the last fifteen years, I have lived in six different locations.

"In the early days, I owned several horses, but my continuous relocations eventually forced me to sell them. I also developed a serious relationship at many of the sites. But when it came time for me to move, the guy was unwilling to come along. As a result, all I do is work. I am professionally successful, but personally restless and unhappy."

I did little more than listen to Daniela. My listening, however, provided the occasion for her to listen to herself, and the 'idleness' of the workshop accelerated this process. It provided her space to step back and see her situation in a new light.

Daniela's ultimate conclusion was that she had thrown away everything she loved most in life in order to meet the demands of her career.

The following day, the last day of the workshop, each participant presented a personal development plan. Daniela, much admired among the group for her professional 'stardom,' surprised everyone by saying she had decided to inform the company she would make one more move. And that move would be her last.

She would then buy a farm and horses and, she hoped, be in a position to develop the long-term relationship she desired.

Several years later, I learned she had done just that.

In idleness, those things that ordinarily shore up our sense of self – normative structures, routines, habits – fall away. Clearing out old forms to make way for the new is a necessary transitional step, but the disorientation and emptiness often experienced in this liminal state can be overwhelming.

Fear is the many-headed 'beast at the garden gate' of idleness, barring us from access to our own creativity. Unless we identify and confront the 'head' we fear most, we may continue indefinitely to cower before the possibilities of creative listening.

Which beastly head most threatens us? Is it the fear that we will be useless, purposeless, deemed without talent, irresponsible, disloyal, or disappointing to others? Is it that we will become lonely and isolated, depressed, crazy, or lost? Or is it that we will be forced to face the big issues of our lives, thus far successfully avoided through relentless busyness?

OVERCOMING THE FEAR OF IDLENESS

You can observe a lot by just watching.

~ Yogi Berra

How are we to slay the dragon, the beast guarding the gate of idleness?

In idleness, fears that lurk just below the surface have the opportunity to rise to consciousness. In fact, the first 'head of the beast' we confront upon entering into an idle state is often the fear of fear itself. So it should not be surprising if our access to the 'garden of idleness,' rich as it is with creative possibilities, seems barred at its very entrance by a fear of confronting our fears.

We must be ready to face our fears, and to move beyond them, before we can bear to be still and listen. Sometimes it takes a crisis, a bottoming out, or perhaps just a winding down from the high-pitched busyness of our lifestyles before we find ourselves willing to be idle.

Ran: From early on, I associated idleness with uselessness, which for me was the most fearsome 'head of the beast.' I remember well the sense of dread I felt during my first visit to a nursing home, where residents with nothing to do sat slumped around the living room in overstuffed chairs.

Proceeding down the hall, I encountered a fragile woman standing 'idly' in front of the elevators. She was offering assistance to the occasional visitor who appeared lost. Having no other way to be useful, she had created this job for herself simply by turning her attention outward to those around her. Through listening, she had found a purpose, and she performed her self-assigned duties with pride and a wonderful smile.

For me, nothing could have been more depressing than the uselessness I witnessed in this woman's fellow residents. And nothing could have been more inspiring than her simple gift.

It is, indeed, reassuring to remember that idleness affords us the opportunity to listen to self, others, and the environment, and that out of this listening will come the answers to whatever our life situation demands.

The courage, even eagerness, to enter into idleness and to hear whatever arises there is the mark of the creative mentality. The one attitude that never fails to open our receptivity and unlock creativity is, "I give up. I relinquish the reins. *I am listening.*" In relinquishing the reins, we relinquish our fears as well.

Cultivating Idleness

We have very little time,
so we must move very slowly.

~ Zen saying

The more we practice quieting consciousness and listening, the easier it becomes. A concrete step we can take in this direction is to implement a 'clutter check' of our lives. How much idleness are we allowing each day? How much time do we spend in 'idle' before we shift into action? Do we need to set aside time daily for the intentional practice of idleness?

For most people attending our *Creative Listening* workshops, the workshop itself represents time they have set aside in their lives to listen to themselves. An improvisational structure we use to focus specifically on this objective is called the 'Check-in Solo.'

Each dancer begins by assuming a shape that identifies what he or she is feeling in the present moment. Listening physically and intuitively into that shape, the dancer waits for an impulse to move. No matter how endless those moments of 'idle' waiting seem, an impulse does come, and then another, and another.

Every second of this one-minute dance, the performer must stay fully committed to making nothing up, but rather to hearing and following into expression whatever comes to consciousness. By remaining open, the performer becomes a transparency for the revelation of his or her own present, inner state.

'Check-in Solos' performed at the beginning of an improvisational session serve to communicate both to ourselves and to others our state of mind. At the end of a session, 'Check-out Solos' do the same. As greetings and farewells, they invite us to pause and take stock before launching into a new phase of action.

Through practice in movement improvisation as well as in our lives, idleness gradually ceases to seem threatening. In fact, instead of a condition fearfully to be avoided, idleness will become our preferred state, a state which opens us up to all the creativity inherent in the improvisational mind.

RECEPTIVITY

The greatest gift you can give another
is the purity of your attention.

~ Richard Moss

What is the key that unlocks our creative muse? More than any one thing, it is the mental state of receptivity. In our improvisational work, we have found three progressive stages of receptivity, which one by one open the way to creative thought and action.

The first stage is giving up on our own personal ability to make things happen, and just *letting go*. The second is turning our focus away from self-interest, or fearful self-concern, towards the practice of *listening*. The third is *embodying* in practice the ideas that emerge from our listening.

STAGE ONE: LETTING GO

When it's dark enough,
you'll be able to see the stars.

~ Charles Beard

Ran: In high school, I just assumed I would attend Oklahoma State, following in my parents' footsteps. But in the spring of my junior year, I bumped into two seniors from the football team. They were filled with excitement about their recent acceptance to Harvard and urged me to apply.

This chance conversation introduced me to a level of academic ambition I had never considered. The next fall, I applied to Harvard and was accepted.

I was used to achieving top grades through hard work, but Harvard was a whole new ballgame. Compared to the rest of my classmates, most of them graduates of elite prep schools, I was an Okie from the sticks. But I knew how to work, and I knuckled down. White-knuckled down.

By the end of the first semester, I found myself completely exhausted. I had hoped to achieve at least a B average. What a shock! Two B-'s and two C+'s.

By the end of the spring term, nothing much had changed. Faced with an overwhelming sense of inadequacy, I hit the wall. I knew I could not work any harder without literally killing myself.

That summer, I took the only path open to me. I just let go. If I could not make the grades, I reasoned, I might as well enjoy the ride. I decided to take full advantage of everything Harvard had to offer. Next year, I would take my courses purely for the joy of learning – and the devil take the grades!

I entered my sophomore year with light-hearted anticipation. Because I had already given up, I felt free. The assigned texts I read for pleasure. Instead of holding back in class discussions, as had been my former practice, I talked so much that one professor held me up as a model for the other students. What did I care what anyone thought? I had nothing left to lose.

That year, I had the time of my life! My grades? By the second semester, most were A's. Later, I went on to graduate magna cum laude, *and then continued on at Harvard for a Ph.D.*

The first stage of receptivity is *letting go*. Its function is to clear the decks. As is true with any behavioral sea change, until we become willing to let go of control, this stage often involves 'hitting the wall.'

Whether we do it instantly or come to it through years of struggle, letting go requires that we lay down willfulness and personal expectations, and shift our basis of operation to a trust in something beyond our own conscious direction of events: the process of listening itself.

Often in this first phase, we are led to reflect upon and redefine our goals. Failure may force us to surrender our pursuit of success, as we have defined it, and perhaps as it is defined in the eyes of most of the world.

It may take a complete breakdown to turn us from the rigidity of our professed aims and ambitions and open our eyes to what actually *is*. Only then, can the power of what *is* begin to change and transform our lives.

STAGE TWO: LISTENING

Nothing happens until something moves.

~ Albert Einstein

Chery: As I was preparing to return to Sarah Lawrence College for my senior year, my father took me aside. He asked if I was feeling nervous at the prospect of teaching my first dance class at Wesleyan to all those college men my own age. Nervous? Scared out of my mind was more like it.

What, exactly, was I afraid of, he wanted to know.

The list was long. That I did not know how to teach dance to male bodies or male psyches; that they would feel awkward and silly with the unfamiliar movement vocabulary; that they would not be challenged; that they would be too challenged; that I would fail to establish the discipline necessary to gain their respect; that I would fail to loosen them up and make them laugh; that I would be unable to convey the artistic, intellectual, spiritual complexity and depth of the material; that, too self-serious, I would not convey its simple delight; that they would run out the doors halfway through the first class and never come back; that they would stay, instead, and I would run out of creative material to teach them ... and on and on.

He listened. Then he asked, "What is it you want to share with your students through these dance classes?"

Only momentarily confounded by the enormity of his question, I launched into a response, equally impassioned and lengthier than my first. When I finished, my father said, "The long and short of it is, you love dance. Is that right?"

I laughed. Yes, that was true.

"Well," he replied, "that love is the real thing you have to share with them. And as for running out of material, just watch them. Listen to them. Look and see what they need. Then make something up to address whatever you see. If they run out of needs, then you run out of material, but not otherwise."

On the first day of classes, I drove up from Sarah Lawrence, so nervous that I sweated right through my dress. When I finally stood at the entrance of the looming theater space, I could just make out my students, lurking shyly in the shadows around the edges of the room. All of them had their required tights modestly bagged halfway down to their knees.

Until that moment, it had never occurred to me how much more courage it took for my students to show up than it did for me. At least I knew the class plan!

Suddenly, my focus shifted from self-concern to concern for each of these daring young men. My own fears retreated. With a sudden thrill of anticipation, I thought, "Hey, guys, not to worry! You're going to love this stuff!"

After letting go, the second stage of receptivity is *listening*. It entails reaching out to something or someone beyond ourselves. Indeed, love and listening are in many ways allied. In improvisation, this shift in attention turns our thought away from fears for self, including concern over personal inadequacy, to ask, "What do *they* need?" or "What does the *dance* need?"

Interest in others or in the work itself crowds out crippling self-consciousness, giving us room to listen. And listening opens up native perspicacity and insight, unavailable through the conscious use of intellect alone.

With listening, comes an inner stillness, an expectancy of good, and a willingness to wait. Patience and persistence, with their hopeful sense of anticipation, are two essential disciplines of creative listening. These unassuming allies of the listening process supply the undergirding necessary to shoulder and carry the weight of this process all the way to fruition.

STAGE THREE: EMBODYING

*Nothing ever becomes real
till it is experienced;
even a proverb is no proverb to you
till your life has illustrated it.*

~ John Keats

One of Chery's colleagues overheard a teacher pressing her student to perform an unaccustomed move. The student was protesting, "I understand it. I just can't do it." The teacher replied, "If you can't do it, then you *don't* understand it."

In order to 'walk our talk,' we have to understand an idea deeply enough to live it. More experientially 'earned' than intellectually 'learned,' embodied understanding actually transforms the self – physically, emotionally, spiritually.

Embodying is tangible 'under-standing' – it puts 'legs' under us that we can stand on. Kinetic understanding, intuitive understanding, spiritual understanding, and what some psychologists have called unconscious understanding, all lead to embodying. They each involve something more than the cognitive intellect.

This third stage of receptivity requires the willingness and courage to act on whatever arises from our deep listening. Colloquially, we call such action 'becoming one with the idea,' 'internalizing it,' 'making the thought our own.' At this level of receptivity, we experience a sense of personal transformation.

None of us ever understands something at the deepest levels of consciousness until we live it. Without this third step, thought cannot cross over into living practice, but remains abstract and theoretical.

It is far easier to profess an understanding of something than to practice an understanding of it. As we will argue later, there is something to be said for forms of education that require this integration of self and idea in life practice.

All of us are certain to fall short of our own professed values and ideals if we are never called upon to exercise the self-discipline, humility, courage, and integrity necessary to live them. In the end, embodying is what keeps us true to ourselves.

THE PRICE OF ENTRY

The greatest obstacle
to discovering the shape of the earth ...
was not ignorance
but the illusion of knowledge.

~ Daniel Boorstin

Receptivity is the open door to creativity. It is the threshold to transformation and change. In many cases, the inexperience of children makes them more receptive than adults to creative imagination. The innocence of their 'beginner's mind' is their creative genius. Adults, as a rule, must win their way back to this receptive state, sometimes at high cost.

To recapitulate, laying down our desire to generate, direct, and control ideas or events is the first payment exacted by our creative muse. The second is turning our attention and energies away from fearful self-concern and towards listening. The final fee is the highest, the price of integrity – walking the talk, embodying the ideas that emerge in consciousness.

There are times, however, when the price of receptivity may seem too high.

Ran: Kate was an obese twenty-year-old college student, who first came to me for counseling over issues of low self-esteem. She was trying to find the confidence to pursue a career as an opera singer.

As is so often the case, deeper issues, lying beneath those of self-esteem, eventually surfaced. Little by little, Kate revealed that she had been sexually abused by her preacher father and was now cutting herself on a regular basis.

During the course of our conversations, Kate made progress. Two images began to emerge, one in stark contrast to the other: Kate's self-image as an opera singer and her self-image as a victim.

She could not, she soon realized, hold onto both images simultaneously. One can-celed out the other. Yet further headway eluded her. To embrace her future would mean leaving go of her past.

Then one night around 2 A.M., I was awakened by a phone call. Kate and her roommate had been taken to the local hospital after a drunken evening of mutual mutilation. She asked for an appointment that morning.

A few short hours later, she sat across from me, recounting the events of the night. I became so nauseated by the details that I could barely make it through the ses-sion. Before Kate finally left the office, however, she announced that she was going to return to her hometown and confront her father for what he had done and her mother for siding with him. Then she was going to move forward with plans to pursue her training as a singer.

I never heard from Kate again. Despite her signs of improvement, I worry to this day that my aseptic reaction made me worse than useless. But Kate taught me a priceless lesson: to be of any help, I must maintain my ability to empathize with my client. And to do this, I must first face and neutralize my own fears.

If we consider all the implications of this story, there are, in fact, several lessons to be garnered.

First, we must have enough humility and self-awareness to recognize when another's struggle feels too close to our own fears. If we cannot gain the perspective and distance necessary to listen, we may have to bow out.

Second, if we elect to remain, we cannot fall for the temptation to believe that the problem is 'out there' somewhere. The problem we face is always the fear within our own consciousness. And, therefore, in this sense, the problem is not 'beyond us.'

Third, focusing exclusively on someone's difficulty may tend to dehumanize him or her in our minds. As an alternative, recognizing aspects we genuinely respect in this individual shifts our perspective, allowing us to stay more present and openhearted. At the very least, remembering that he or she is a fellow human being will help us maintain our empathy.

Fourth, we can overcome any fears, even the most intimidating, if we begin with small enough steps. Taking on less frightening situations at first, will allow us to develop the confidence and acquire the experience needed to prepare us for more demanding challenges. As in the case of koans, repeatedly facing our own fears and moving through them will free us to focus on the concerns of others.

Achieving a state of receptivity is no small task for any of us. It requires courage and humility, the willingness to grapple with fear in ourselves, in order to attend non-judgmentally the concerns of another. At times, this may seem a stiff price for simple receptivity, but paying this price is the precursor to every serviceable work, the principal thing enabling us to be useful to the world, even creative.

WILL

It is not my experience
that we are here to fix the world....
I think we are here
so the world can change us.

~ Cheri Huber

The question of will is central to creativity, especially as it affects the delicate balance between vitality and surrender that is the mark of the improvisational mind. Successful improvisation, whether in art or in life, hangs on the differences between a willful, a willing, and a will-less act.

THE WILL TRILOGY

The trouble with our conscious mind
is that it tries too hard.

~ R. Reid Wilson

In the English language, the term 'will' is used in many ways. Here, we want to specify our own uses of the word 'will' and its derivatives – both positive and negative.

In the practice of creative listening, we have found that 'willfulness' and 'will-lessness' are really two sides of the same counterfeit coin. But 'will-ingness' is something else altogether – the true currency.

Chery & Ran: Nicole, a dance major at a religiously based university, was an intelligent, beautiful, talented, and decidedly organized young woman. Her goals in life were ambitious, and she moved towards them with resolve. Still, she was very thoughtful to those around her and close to her family. She had always been an obedient child.

When it came to dance, Nicole was highly directed, even willful at times. But in social situations, she admitted, she often yielded her will to the desires of others and could become almost too passive and submissive.

In a Creative Listening workshop she attended, Nicole identified these two sides of her character via an improvisational structure called 'The Will Trilogy.' In this structure, three dancers perform three improvisations sequentially.

For the first piece, one dancer is given the assignment to be willful, the second dancer to be will-less, and the third to be willing. When the first piece is completed, the same dancers shift their roles and perform a second improvisation. For the third dance, the roles shift again.

In all three pieces, the dancers begin in physical contact with one another. For each dancer to persist with his or her role, and keep it distinct from the other roles, requires real focus of attention. If they are successful, however, the improvisations are unusually entertaining and often poignant.

After performing 'The Will Trilogy,' it became clear to Nicole that she typically conducted her work life as the 'willful dancer' and her social life as the 'will-less dancer.' But there was an anomalous aspect to her social life – a boyfriend.

When she and her boyfriend were together, Nicole normally called the shots. For the most part, this worked out well. Chris was an amiable young man who supported Nicole's professional aspirations and shared her spiritual convictions. He was perfect for her, she felt, except for his reluctance to say anything to her about his inner life.

Nicole had tried being willful, protesting when he did not talk. She had tried being will-less, retreating into her own silence. Both roles were familiar, but neither approach satisfied.

It was through dancing 'The Will Trilogy' that Nicole realized she had a third option. She could again voice her desire for greater communication, but this time be willing to listen to Chris's response, even if words were not his medium of choice.

She opened herself up to the possibility that he might be more comfortable convey-ing his thoughts and feelings directly – through the way he treated her, the activi-ties they shared in common, the values he demonstrated in his interactions with others, and the mores by which he led his life.

If she wanted communication with Chris, Nicole concluded, she would have to be willing to listen to however he chose to 'speak.'

Each of the three 'will' mindsets has a different quality. And this quality determines how they interact with the world.

Both willful and will-less attitudes are fearful at base. One is overbearing, the other, spineless.

Willfulness is active, which is positive, but it is also controlling and dis-trustful. If willful, we spend our time and energy pushing the world around or outlining some desired outcome.

Will-lessness, the polar opposite, reflects a passive attitude. In this center-less state, we are apt to become submissive to domination, addiction, and apathy.

In contrast, willingness represents neither the ego-directed position of willfulness nor the ego-defeated position of will-lessness. It is a *responsive* position.

Willingness is self-contained, but receptive. It has the energy of willful-ness, but without its aggressive rigidity. It has the yielding quality of will-lessness, but without its lifeless passivity. The willing state of mind neither dominates nor is dominated, is neither master nor slave.

If willing, we have a sense of trust and confidence. We can step into the unknown, without the need for dictating or having foreknowledge of the specific forms in which the future will emerge.

TRUST

The great act of faith
is when man decides
that he is not God.

~ William James

The improvisational mind fosters creativity through trust, not through willfulness or will-lessness with their underlying fears. In its freedom from fear, trust becomes the power behind willingness. This power involves a singular combination of resolve and surrender.

Trust in the improvisational process is at the heart of creative listening. It is what enables us to be patient, to wait on intuition, and then to follow its lead without active or passive resistance. Distrust of the improvisational process is the weakness underlying will-lessness and is the hidden fire at the heart of willful desire.

Faced with a challenging situation, if trusting, we listen calmly both inwardly and outwardly for direction, and act accordingly. If will-less, we are apt to be overwhelmed by external influences and lose our inner direction. If willful, we are liable to react to a challenge with force, jumping out of our own lane to direct and dictate everyone else's path.

INNER RESOURCES

Long sought without,
but found within.

~ John Greenleaf Whittier

Willfulness may appear to be strength, but it is actually uncertainty in disguise. It signals the presence of fear. Whenever we lack confidence in the ability of listening to generate the best solution, we are likely to prescribe a particular outcome in advance, one constrained to fit our limited vision.

Moreover, if we look behind any of our unsatisfied, willful desires we often discover we are seeking an external answer, a physical symbol – person, place, or thing – in an attempt to satisfy a deeper internal need. If this is the case, our externally derived answers prove to be just temporary fixes.

Lasting answers are found only in listening deeply. What we want is already present within us. And that is the ability to listen and hear the 'just right' intuition or idea for every unfolding moment. This listening reveals ideas that are present but unseen, and brings them into view.

If we begin an improvisation or any kind of project with willingness instead of willfulness, we act as if the project were complete before we begin. Our intention as improviser, therefore, is not to *force* or *will* the outcome, but to *discover* the 'dance' as if it were already there, perfect and entire.

SURRENDER VS. SUBMISSION

Such is life,
falling over seven times
and getting up eight.

~ Roland Barthes

But what about will-lessness, with its feeling of inertia and hopelessness? Is the 'submission' at the core of will-lessness the same as the 'surrender' we experience with willingness? Not at all.

As in the case of willfulness, will-lessness is a reaction to fear. However, as the polar opposite of the aggressive hyper-activity of willfulness, will-lessness manifests itself in mental and emotional flatness, deadness, and ultimately despair. In this state, our energies are sapped by a feeling of impotence.

By contrast, willingness indicates unfettered expectancy. It reflects a sense of potential. In this state, we are keenly alert and aware. Willingness requires the surrender of self-will, but not of mindfulness, discernment, or energy.

Chery: My brother made the high school wrestling team in his junior year. He was tall for a wrestler, but an energetic, hard working, spirited team player. Yet despite rigorous dedication and training, by the end of the season, Thor had won only a few matches.

Because wrestling requires such resolute focus, grueling effort, and individual courage, the pressure at these competitions was intense. Thor often felt nauseous before his match. Once he even threw up on the sidelines.

The final match of the season was at home. It was expected to be a good one, and everyone was stoked to win. Our parents and all Thor's friends would be there.

He knew this was his last chance. He very much wanted to make a good showing and to support his team. But all he could remember was something his girlfriend had said to him a few days before, "Why don't you ever win?"

Later that day, all the wrestlers weighed in. Thor's opponent came in overweight. Normally in a case like this, the overweight wrestler is disqualified, and the team with the qualified wrestler wins the match by default. Nonetheless, the qualifying wrestler does have the option to waive these rights and agree to the contest anyway.

Thor wanted to wrestle. He wanted to win on his own, not by default. But when the question was put to him, his first concern was his responsibility to his teammates. Because he already had the win by default, a match win would be a victory only for himself. And if he lost, it would count against the team.

"I want to wrestle," he told his teammates. "But it's up to you. I will go with whatever you guys decide." Their vote was unanimous – no confidence. And who could blame them?

There remained one final possibility. After the official team matches were over and the scores tallied, Thor could wrestle his opponent in an exhibition match. Although the statistics of their match would be recorded, the score would not officially count.

This moment was Thor's nadir. Girlfriend, teammates, no one expected him to succeed. What did he have to lose?

The next day in the high school bulletin, his wrestling coach posted the results of the match. It had been a tough competition, but the team had won by a slim margin.

And this win was particularly sweet. It had meant the difference between a winning and a losing season.

Yet the most remarkable part of the match, the bulletin went on to say, was the exhibition match. In this match, Thor had pinned his opponent in twenty-two seconds. It was the fastest pin in his weight class in the history of the school.

As Janis Joplin sings in *Me and Bobby McGee*, there is a freedom in "nothing left to lose." This freedom is not submission to a state of fear, but the surrender of fear itself. Instead of trying to battle its way out of a critical situation, our ego bottoms out, lets go, and fear falls away. In this fearless state, we just focus – right here, right now – and listen.

Neither our energy nor our regulation of that energy is lost when we give up willfulness or will-lessness. In fact, energy and its regulation are found in their surrender. Turning from fear, we are able to hear and respond freely to the intuitive, inner voice that provides exact guidance for when and how to act, guidance that comes as a direct result of our yielding up self-will.

WILL AND CREATIVITY

There is nothing
as dangerous as having an idea,
if it's the only idea you have.

~ Bill O'Hanlon

How do these three mental states – willful, will-less, and willing – compare for the person or performer experiencing them? How do they compare in the experience of an audience or others observing them in action?

Willfulness often brings a temporary and sometimes impressive energy to a performance, activity, or group project. Eventually, however, the rigidity it also produces becomes apparent. An individual acting willfully can become narrowly single-minded, repetitive, or insensitive in his or her action choices. Furthermore, his or her domination over co-participants can limit everyone's creative explorations and discoveries. To an observer, such a person resembles a bull in a china closet.

Likewise, someone acting will-lessly may seem at first a good improviser, in this case, open and receptive. But again a shallowness of range is eventually revealed, and the individual's dependency on others for innovation and energy becomes deadening. To the observer, such a person appears limp and spiritless.

Artists and other creative thinkers regularly speak of 'the work,' the project itself, as taking over the decision-making process at a certain point. Though keenly alert and responsive, not passive in the will-less sense, the creator feels almost like an observer of the creative process, moved by something beyond him or herself. This experience, of course, is synonymous with the heightened listening state we call being 'willing.'

For both the performer and the observer, it may take some practice to become adept at detecting the differences among these three states of mind. In the long run, however, an alertness to these distinctions will be helpful in discerning in ourselves and others the mental qualities that best promote creativity.

CREATIVITY AND FREEDOM

No man is free who is not master of himself.

~ Epictetus

Our consideration of will ultimately leads us to reflect on the relationship of will to freedom, of freedom to discipline, and of both freedom and discipline to creativity.

Chery: *Friends often remark on the level of discipline in my life, and today this characteristic seems to come naturally. But, in fact, it was an attribute hard won.*

I was raised by energetic, accomplished parents with high standards and expectations for their children, yet with a permissive approach to parenting. As a small child, I enjoyed the liberty of following my own inclinations and finding my own internal directions. But, I was soon to discover, there were troubling aspects to this freedom.

One of the most disconcerting was the difficulty I encountered in disciplining myself, when I had been taught so little about obeying anyone else. This was not to say that I was an unruly child. Far from it. But by and large, I obeyed because I wanted to obey, I wanted to please.

I found it a mystery how others could lay aside their desires and obey externally imposed authority against their own inner inclinations. And similarly, I found it difficult to discipline my own actions contrary to my feelings. I could do it, but it always involved a hard struggle.

Like most children, I loved my parents and wished to make them proud, and they continued to support me as they always had. As I approached the seventh grade, however, and homework became heavier, I realized that a higher level of self-discipline would be required of me to meet the academic standards of excellence my parents expected.

How was I to achieve this self-discipline? How was I to learn self-government all on my own?

At this point in my life, I attempted to apply a strict, willful self-discipline in performing my studies and chores. This worked pretty well for a while; but as it was born of fear, it had a dark side.

Worn out by the willfulness with which I had spurred myself to action and bound myself to restraint, I eventually found the opposite kicked in – will-lessness. Though it was clear something was needed for my recuperation from all that willful effort, this was not it. Will-lessness had a certain quality of self-indulgence, but it was no more caring or self-respectful than willfulness had been. For years, I swung back and forth between these polar opposites.

It was in my sophomore year in college that I first glimpsed a way out. In my dance composition class, students received weekly assignments to create short dance 'studies.' For me, creating these studies was anguishing. I felt nothing I came up with was ever good enough. Every assignment was an ordeal, and I labored and fretted over these minor creations for hours on end.

One Sunday afternoon, finally exhausted by this struggle, I made a decision. Instead of marshalling all my energies and willing myself to make another piece, I would surrender. I would **yield.** *I would put one foot in front of the other, get myself over to the studio, and just do it.*

All the drama and angst went out of the choreographic process. Emotionally, it felt surprisingly bland, easy, sort of gray. No ego. No passion. Just focus.

I set borders. I gave myself thirty minutes to make the study – twenty minutes to come up with the raw material and ten minutes to arrange and practice it until I had it memorized. Whatever was finished by the end of that time, I would show in class Monday morning.

I wasted no time, because there was no time to waste. I took what movement came to me without agonizing over its merits. I got into the studio, put the dance together, got out.

And this was the big surprise: Monday morning, the feedback on this little piece was positive. In fact, it was more positive than usual. There was a freshness about the work that people liked. As always, I was given some suggestions for improving it, and that was that. No big deal.

But for me, that little, gray half-hour in a basement studio was a very big deal, the beginning of a whole new way of work and life. It was among my earliest steps towards the discipline and freedom of the improvisational mind.

The exercise of willfulness is often mistaken for freedom. "I just want to do what I want to do!" But the latitude of permissiveness is not synonymous with the freedom of self-governance.

Freedom is complex. It involves borders and control. "What I want" is not always so easy to determine. Even when feeling we are certain of our wants, we may be self-deceived. Or later, upon reflection, our desires of the moment may prove short-sighted. As if that were not confusing enough, what we think are our desires may not be our desires at all, but someone else's desires for us, which we have internalized.

Furthermore, whenever we attempt to listen to 'our inner voice,' we may encounter more than one. One of these voices may express a momentary impulse. Another may urge us towards long-term goals. A third may impel us to act from a higher moral sense of right.

The freedom of the improvisational mind involves a delicate and disciplined balance. Learning to distinguish between willfulness, will-lessness, and willingness in improvisational practice is an invaluable aid to walking that fine line of liberty.

As we observe in human society, freedom and self-governance go hand in hand. Only through self-governance, do we find true freedom and access to our own unique creative voice.

DISTRACTION

That which hinders your task
__is__ your task.

~ Sanford Meisner

The distractions of fear that cross our path daily are numerous and often subtle and seductive. But to realize our creative potential, we must learn to stay focused, to maintain our mental alertness and listen. Resisting the temptation to become sidetracked requires a continuous, disciplined presence of mind.

Three of the most common distractions in the practice of creative listening are a sense of *personal responsibility* to generate creativity, a need to *control others* in order to succeed, and a fear of *judgment*.

PERSONAL RESPONSIBILITY

All forms of fear produce fatigue.

~ Bertrand Russell

The first distraction is the fear that it is our personal responsibility to come up with answers and creative solutions, instead of simply listening for and receiving them.

Chery: In my senior year as a dance major at Sarah Lawrence, I had a packed schedule. Most of my course load was devoted to dance. Beyond that, obligations included serving as head of the dance students' organization and making weekly trips from New York to Connecticut to teach my class at Wesleyan.

To complete my academic requirements for graduation, one more course from a field outside my major was requisite. Of the courses that drew my interest, only two fit into my schedule. Both were in high demand. The first course to which I applied, being the larger of the two, seemed the more likely choice. But I did not get in.

The teacher of the second course was highly regarded on campus and popular with students, despite a reputation for exacting assignments and stiff workloads. The class was limited to fifteen students. When I finally secured an interview with the professor, the end of the enrollment process was near.

Watching the late afternoon sun streaming through the windows, I sat waiting for the professor to appear. There seemed to be no room, no room in my schedule for courses and no room in courses for me. I sought to calm my almost desperate state of mind. Listening inwardly, I heard the words, "There is always room for light."

The professor arrived and got straight to the point. "I have three spaces left in this course and thirteen applicants for them ahead of you," he said. "Most of these students are majors in my department. You have never taken a single course in my field. Tell me, why should I accept you over any of them?"

I knew instantly that never in a million years could I come up with a rationally compelling answer. I closed my eyes and listened. What I heard come out of my mouth was this: "In my field, we don't judge people so much by what they say, but by what they do. I know how sincere my desire is to succeed in this course and how hard I will work. Judge me on that."

He looked at me a long time in silence. Then he said quietly, "Ms. Cutler, you are accepted."

In creative listening, our responsibility is not to come up with answers, ideas, or solutions. In fact, we must actively resist the temptation to do so.

Our job is to maintain the improvisational mind – to keep thought free from the distractions of fear; to pay close attention to whatever thoughts, feelings, and intuitions are generated by listening; and to follow through with these intuitions. In other words, to reiterate an earlier affirmation, our single responsibility lies in our ability to respond.

Although this responsive approach precludes a willful initiation of action, responsiveness, as we have said, does not imply passivity. We act in improvisation, but we do so by responding to intuitions that surface from our deep listening, not by imposing our thoughts, fears, or desires upon a situation.

This discipline, so counter-intuitive to a commonsense understanding of responsibility, involves, first and foremost, maintaining a state of quiet alertness – a balance of inner and outer awareness. Only once this mentality is established, and not before, do we follow through with action.

In improvisation, taking it upon ourselves to personally determine and decide matters is not being responsible. Indeed, to jump the gun and act before we listen is the very definition of irresponsibility.

CONTROLLING OTHERS

Everyone wants to change humanity,
but nobody wants to change himself.

~ Leo Tolstoy

Another common temptation that might cause us to lose focus and cease listening is the fear that, unless we control others, our endeavors may not succeed.

Chery: When I returned to Alaska for my thirtieth High School reunion, I asked a number of my classmates what was the most important thing they had learned since graduation. Alan, always funny and often incisively perceptive, offered a particularly memorable answer.

He had learned a good number of things, he said, but if he had to choose, he would choose this one: Men feel they have to be right; women feel they have to fix men.

This was Alan's story: "In my first marriage, I felt my wife was always trying to fix me. But I, being a man, always had to 'be right.'

"After that marriage failed, I met Heather, and something unexpected happened. She did not try to change me. She just loved me and loved me and loved me.

"Then one day it occurred to me that maybe there were a few things I could and should change about myself. So I did."

In any intimate relationship, democratic group project, or movement improvisation, our job is not to control how the other players act. Minding our own business in this regard is essential. Instead, our role in relation to others is to listen and respond to them in the spirit of cooperation and respect, not to second-guess or direct them.

But what if *they* are not listening with an improvisational mind? What do we do then? Just this: when others fail to listen, we must listen all the more.

Whenever we listen, there is an unmistakable quality, a candor, a genuineness evident in our performance. This listening in the face of others' non-listening commonly has the effect of allowing, indeed enabling them to listen better.

But whether others' attention improves or not, if *we* persist in listening, we can rest assured that the project or improvisation will unfold successfully. In fact, if we continue to listen in cases where someone else is 'out of it,' things often work out in especially surprising and unexpected ways.

When another is not listening, we need not be concerned with protecting the integrity of the improvisation or our own integrity within it. Our listening and the resulting truthfulness of our responses will do that work.

Listening enables us to stay in touch with ourselves, with our own inner voice and sense of direction, as well as with others and the circumstances around us. Listening without fear preserves our integrity, and that integrity is the one power we always have when we are confused or threatened and everything is on the line.

Transparency is what best elucidates and convinces. We serve any group project best not by manipulating or dominating others, a sure sign that fear is in control, but by gaining dominion over our fear and acting from that fearless base.

Are there exceptions to this rule not to take charge? Yes, of course. Snatching a child from the path of an oncoming car is an obvious real-life example. In such a case, to suspend momentarily our non-directiveness of others, and if necessary use physical force to protect those in danger, reflects good listening.

In improvisation, we are always paying attention and responding to three areas simultaneously – self, other, environment. Usually, we try to keep our awareness of all three areas in some kind of balance. However, it is necessary at times to prioritize our attention and actions. An imbalance of attention is appropriate in instances where one area, such as that of the environment, presents a danger to someone's safety.

In small ways, this momentary imbalance happens all the time in improvisation. For short periods, it is natural and often useful. If the imbalance in our perspective persists, however, it will eventually jeopardize the appropriateness of our actions.

FEAR OF JUDGMENT

Tell me what is it that you plan to do
with your one wild and
precious life.

~ Mary Oliver

Of all the distractions we face in improvisation or in any other creative endeavor, the fear of judgment is among the most aggressive.

Chery: Wendy was a dance major at Wesleyan. After graduating, she worked in New York City for a time, doing office work while dancing and choreographing on the side. Eventually, she made a sudden decision to return to school for a graduate degree in dance.

As she perused entrance requirements and application deadlines, she was startled to realize that one university was holding an audition the very next day, the only audition offered for next year's program. In haste, she called to place her name on their applicant list.

When she arrived on campus, Wendy was expecting to participate in a dance technique audition. To her astonishment, she discovered everyone else was nervously rehearsing the solo which each candidate had choreographed to perform before the panel of judges.

Wendy had no dance. And it was now or never.

When it came time for her solo, Wendy presented herself before the judges and explained her plight. She stated that instead of foregoing her opportunity to apply, she would perform an improvisation. The other applicants in the room looked on aghast.

She took her place on the floor and began with the quiet, centered, inner focus she had learned from her study of improvisation as an undergraduate. When the dance concluded, she stepped up before the judges for their response.

At first, no one spoke. Then one judge asked, "Are you, by any chance, from Wesleyan?"

Astonished, Wendy blurted out, "How did you know?"

"Well," the judge replied, "we have all just watched you create something out of nothing!"

As it turned out, Wendy eventually chose another institution for her Masters study, but in the years that followed, her story became an inspiration for Wesleyan dance students and professors alike.

In the midst of the creative act, allowing our mind to wander to concerns over how our project or performance will be judged can cripple creative integrity. It scatters our attention and deflects our energies. During the creative process, therefore, the single most effective thing we can do to assure a successful outcome is to stay mentally present and focused on our central assignment: to quiet fear and listen.

A great deal of self-discipline is required, especially at first, to trust the improvisational process. It is generally only with practice and experience that we learn to focus on process, rather than product.

And why does this work, why does focusing upon the creative process produce the best product? Because, as we stated early on, the process of an improvisation, like the process of living itself, actually *is* its product. And the product of any creation, improvisation or not, is the direct manifestation of the mentality and thought processes that produced it.

LITERALISM

To say to the painter
that Nature is to be taken as she is,
is to say to the player
that he may sit on the piano.

~ James Whistler

Sometimes in our workshops, participants confront us with the question, "What is the difference between 'play-acting' and 'creative listening?'" The difference, we believe, is subtle but critical. Consider the following example:

Chery & Ran: *One day, a group of our workshop participants asked if they could improvise a piece around a predetermined dramatic theme – not an approach to which we normally subscribe.*

They took the stage and began to portray their idea through mimed interaction. Here, the dancers were engaging in what we call 'play-acting,' depicting their theme in a form of 'dumb show' without actually listening to what was going on with their movements, thoughts, and feelings at that present moment.

As a result, their characterizations tended to be broad, without nuance, and their plot, predictable. The audience just sat back, awaiting the end they saw coming.

Then all at once, one of the performers, frustrated by the relentlessness of her role, broke away from the unspoken script with a reaction completely unexpected, yet altogether true to her character and its circumstances. In this moment, she actually listened and responded to what she heard – inside and out.

Instantly, the whole dance came alive. No one knew what to expect, neither dancers nor audience. The audience sat up, engaged. It was as if they were witnessing the naked thought processes of everyone onstage. The drama was suddenly raw, uncanned, open to surprise and revelation.

This brilliant break lasted only a minute. But the difference between play-acting and this live improvisational response was so striking, that it illustrated vividly for the audience the distinction between making something up and actual creative listening.

PANTOMIME

*I laugh when I hear
the fish in the water
is thirsty.*

~ Kabir

Pantomimic gesture is a form of literalism. To the beginning improviser, pantomime may seem to provide a safe, recognizable vocabulary. But inherent in it are certain limitations and problems.

In essence, pantomime is a cognitive sign language, a kind of choreographed, set vocabulary of meaning. As such, it is narrowly prescriptive, allowing neither audience nor performers much range of interpretation or response.

In set choreography, where the dance reflects a predetermined vision and message, pantomimic gesture may provide narrative clarity and play an important organizational role in helping the story along. Its effects are restrictive, narrowly defining the import of the dance, but they are meant to be so.

In group improvisation *without* a predetermined script, however, these effects are not so desirable. Even one literal gesture tends to dictate the dance, its direction and its meaning.

Confining the dance to a single level of interpretation or reference, this literalism restricts the choices and creativity of all the dancers. Likewise, literalism limits opportunities for the audience to perceive wider or deeper meanings of their own.

Nevertheless, pantomimic gesture, although problematic, is not prohibited in dance improvisation. If used with conscious awareness, sensitivity, and integrity, it can be employed effectively by the skillful performer, one who knows how to remain open to unexpected possibilities and incongruous perspectives even in the face of a hackneyed idiom.

There are also analogies of pantomime that show up in everyday life. One simple example is that of the rhetorical question, where the questioner typically has in mind an answer so narrowly prescribed that he or she cannot hear the answers others offer, no matter how appropriate or insightful?

In such a case, the question is actually a 'pantomime' of a question. The questioner appears to be calling for answers, but in practice shuts out any answer that diverges from the scripted one already in his or her mind.

Literalism, closely allied with fundamentalism, works much the same way as pantomime. All three – literalism, fundamentalism, and pantomime – are strict and exacting and leave little room for deviation. In all three cases, only a selective form of listening, if any at all, is usually involved.

Body Language

*Personality is an unbroken string
of successful gestures.*

~ F. Scott Fitzgerald

Charades is a guessing game employing pantomime as a language. It exemplifies the use of literal gesture as a means of communication.

Some players are more adept at this language than others. Similarly, some cultures employ gesture more richly in daily conversation than other cultures. But to one degree or another, all people use movement as a means of communication, most commonly in the form of gestures, such as beckoning with an arm or pressing a forefinger to the lips.

Body postures and facial expressions are also basic to what we call 'body language.' In comparison to culturally codified gestures, postures tend to be more subtle and complex, and consequently more difficult to read and interpret accurately.

Slumped shoulders and a caved chest, for instance, may express anything from dejection to weariness to secrecy to fear. By contrast, shoulders
thrown back and chest puffed forward may indicate cheerfulness, robust-
ness, preening, defensiveness, or pride.

*Chery: During our training for certification in Laban Movement Analysis, my class-
mates and I were ferried to Seattle's famous Pike Street Market on several field trips.*

*Our teachers assigned us the task of following behind different customers and
assuming their body postures. Our job was to record the postures and gestures of
those we shadowed, as well as documenting the feeling states we experienced in
mirroring each individual's movements.*

*My fellow students and I reported with some astonishment that we immediately
registered vivid mental and emotional attitudes when taking on each new physical
configuration, revealing how graphically body alignment conjures up meaning.*

*We realized then that simple kinetic empathy, as we experienced in this exercise, is
one reason why theater and dance have such an impact on an audience. The audience virtually feels the action in their own bodies and reads into the movement an
interpretation of the performers' mental states.*

HOW DANCE SIGNIFIES MEANING

*Our expression and our words never coincide,
which is why
the animals don't understand us.*

~ Ortega Y. Gasset

Most members of an audience are not cognizant of how they are 'reading'
movement onstage, but whether viewing choreography or improvisation,
they are somehow making meaning of what they see.

Throughout history, dancers have explored a wide range of rich and sophisticated ways in which movement conveys thought. Chery's former colleague, Susan Foster, identifies four such ways.[1]

In the late Renaissance, Foster states, everything presented onstage was understood to be metaphor. For instance, the actions of a dancer parading the stage in a costume draped with grapes might signify the political activities of a French province famous for its vineyards.

In neoclassical proscenium theater ballets, dancers communicated dramatic narrative through pantomime, even to the degree of miming every word in a sentence, such as: "Please don't shoot my swans." This was, indeed, a form of charades.

In American expressionist modern dance, like the choreography of Martha Graham, dancers suggested inner psychological states through non-literal movement. Although more abstract than pantomime, this choreographic form could eloquently convey emotional resonance.

In contemporary, postmodern dance, movement is presentational rather than representational. Dancers do not intend to refer to or signify other events or emotions. Movement is just movement – movement for movement's sake.

As we can see from this brief sketch of Foster's categories, literalism is one avenue open to us, but it is far from the only way we can employ and interpret movement in the communication of thought and emotion. When attempting to translate intangible thought into tangible form, however, the seductive lure of literalism is always with us.

---

1   Susan Leigh Foster, *Reading Dancing: Bodies and Subjects in Contemporary American Dance*, University of California Press, 1986.

'One Liners'

To name is to destroy,
to suggest is to create.

~ Stephane Mallarme

In our workshops, one of the ways we bring attention to the problem of literalism is through an improvisational structure we call 'One Liners.' This structure introduces the use of words into the dances.

Words are highly seductive. They tend to elicit literal responses in beginning improvisers. So we begin the introduction of 'text' gently.

One person stands before the audience and delivers a single phrase or sentence, such as, "Flying by the seat of my pants," then joins the audience. Two to five dancers take positions onstage and perform a piece.

The dancers' assignment is to allow the phrase to reverberate in their minds but not to respond literally to the words or images. For instance, if the sentence has the word 'dog' in it, they would do well to avoid literal gestures such as cocking a bent leg.[2]

Instead, dancers are directed to attend the abstract qualities of whatever beginning positions they assume and allow the improvisation to unfold from there. Although the postures and gestures in the piece make no direct reference to the sentence, the words remain inexorably in the consciousness of performers and audience alike, subtly coloring both their movements in and perceptions of the dance.

Essentially, this structure is a juxtaposition of two or more levels of meaning. At least one level is introduced though the movement and another through the text. This overlay of mostly random, unrelated ideas creates or discovers unexpected relationships.

---

2   Of course, there are no absolute rules in art. In the hands of a skilled and subtle improviser, this literal gesture could be wonderfully funny.

'One Liners' is a subtle structure that usually requires some practice. Once performers get the hang of it, however, they often produce unusual and surprising pieces. They begin to experience the creative freshness of unexpected juxtapositions that free their work from the one-dimensional flatness of literalism.

CONVEYING THE INTANGIBLE

If you don't live it,
it don't come out of your horn.

~ Charlie Parker

Ran: There is a story in the Zen tradition of a young acolyte seeking enlightenment. He had heard many stories of a particular master, renowned for his magnificent pottery. The pots he created, it was said, were of transcendent beauty.

The young student had never seen this master's work, nor could he find anyone who owned a single piece. He began to wonder why.

"Maybe his reputation is just a legend," he thought. "Maybe this 'master' is nothing more than a myth. Or worse: a fraud."

The young man decided he would have to find out for himself. He traveled to a remote mountain village, where the master was reputed to live, and was directed by the villagers up a steep, rough path to a small hut.

As the young man approached the dwelling, he came upon piles of disfigured pots littered about the premises.

"With so many failures," he pondered, "what kind of master can this be?"

The youth made his way as quietly as he could up to the open door. As he peered inside, he saw a room completely bare except for a potter's wheel. No pots anywhere.

An unassuming figure, wizened with age, sat at the wheel working. He was so absorbed that he seemed not to have heard the stranger's approach. In silent, perfect concentration, he began to turn the wheel and shape the clay before him.

As the young man watched, a shape of the most astonishing loveliness rose up between the old man's hands. It was like a living thing, the most exquisite object he had ever beheld.

When the potter had finished, he sat back and observed the pot. The young man stood in the doorway spellbound. Then with one swift gesture, the potter grasped the pot, mashed it in his hands, and hurled it out the door.

"What have you done?" the young man gasped, stumbling into the room. "I have come all this way to see your magnificent works, and what have you to show? Nothing! Nothing but globs of clay! Where is your life's work?" he demanded angrily.

The old man looked at him quietly. Then he stretched out his empty hands.

The forms of expression any idea may take are not themselves the state of mind that produced these forms. The forms are only the wake of that idea, as it moves like a craft through the waters of the mind.

How to convey a state of mind or any conceptual reality using finite forms, such as clay, words, or movement, without resorting to literalism, is a perpetual dilemma in all artistic, psychological, and spiritual disciplines.

As difficult as this translation of thought into expression may be, however, it is only the initial hurdle. Once an idea or experience has been rendered into a formal language, there is still the danger that an observer will misunderstand the creator's intent through literal interpretation.

After all, however perfect, a symbol is not its subject. The *word* 'tree' is not the tree itself. A pot is not enlightenment.

As a prime illustration of the problem in conveying the intangible, a debate exists in the field of dance over where the 'dance' itself lies. 'Materialists' contend that a dance exists in the movements themselves, and therefore is preserved through the replication of its exact choreographic form. 'Idealists' counter that a dance resides in the ideas of the dance. For the idealist, the dance is preserved as long as the essence and meaning of the dance are captured, even if the exact steps are not.

We side with the idealists. In the same way that the *word* 'tree' is not a *tree*, we contend that a *dance* is not its *steps*. How does the idealist, then, transmit a dance to another person – whether to a dancer learning the dance or to an audience watching its performance?

This quandary is illustrated by our experience with the Chinese riddle: How can we hold water, fire, and wind in paper?

Chery: *Ran had retained no memory of the riddle, but it remained indelible in my mind, because I saw in it the analogy of a dilemma I faced daily in my academic life.*

That dilemma was how to capture and convey an elemental, living experience, such as dance (water, fire, wind), in language (paper) adequate to communicate its educational value to powerful administrators who may know and care little about the field.

The first hurdle the department faced was to resist explaining what dancers do by reverting to literal description. Dance is not just steps, "one-two-three, one-two-three."

The second challenge was to discourage administrators from imposing a literal interpretation of their own, such as assuming that dance is merely physical movement – all body and no mind.

My colleagues and I sought to accomplish both these tasks, first by listening to the language administrators used, as shaped by their interests, aims, and values, and then by talking about dance in terms that spoke to these concerns.

By presenting dance in terms familiar and vital to the administration, we hoped to steer their understanding of dance and its educational possibilities away from the reductive and towards the field's natural alliance with the central concerns of a university.

The third challenge was to uphold the artistic and educational vision of the department in those areas that were neither valued by, nor easily translated for, a nonpractitioner. This task proved to be the most arduous.

The tack my colleagues and I took was to strive for excellence in both performance and scholarship, without sacrificing one for the other. This we achieved by centering our curriculum on a third aspect of dance: creativity. The performative and the scholarly aspects were then positioned not as competing directions of study, but as twin buttresses to this central spire. And, of course, learning to think creatively, a valued pursuit in any academic field, was universally respected.

This paradigm of dance education required maintaining, on a limited budget, high standards in all areas of the department, and doing so in the face of many divergent opinions (sometimes within the department, but mostly without) on the nature of dance.

Over the years, in presenting our case to the administration for support of the dance program, catching the living stuff of dance in – or on – paper was a virtual impossibility. What we could do, however, was present compelling, logical arguments, draw analogies to other fields of study, and provide traces of objective evidence of dance's effects, like the trees provide evidence of the wind.

Ultimately, the only vessel that can adequately communicate a thing of life is our own lives. Living and practicing the intangible ideas we hope to preserve and communicate is the one certain way to capture them in a non-reductive way.

In the end, to convey the virtues and value of dance, one has to dance.

LITERALISM IN LIFE PRACTICE

In a war of ideas
it is people who get killed.

~ Stanislaw J. Lec

We face literalism not just in art, but in the larger world as well. Some form of literalism or fundamentalism appears in virtually every religion or ideology.

What we mean by 'literalism' is a strict adherence to the letter of the word, to the forms by which a belief is represented or expressed. With literalism, there is only one possible level of interpretation.

At one time or another, most of us have succumbed to the danger inherent in literalism – inflexibility, dogmatism, and the unwillingness to listen. Dogmatic adherence to any position inevitably alienates rather than communicates.

Ran: After over ten years of workaholic study at Harvard, I resolved not to subject my own students to this same kind of torment. With youthful energy and idealism – and a large measure of naïveté – I set out to turn the educational system on its head.

I remember the first-day-of-class hush as I walked into my maiden course at Smith College in 1967. Without speaking, I took a seat at the head of a long table. Fifteen young women looked expectantly towards me. I looked down at my hands and remained silent.

As I later learned, some were thinking, "Poor guy, he's too shy to start." Others, a little awed, assumed I was praying or maybe meditating. The minutes ticked by, and a few students began to fidget with their papers, while others buried themselves in their books and notes. After ten or fifteen minutes, the tension became almost unbearable.

Finally, a hand went up marionette-like, and a timid voice inquired, "Is it permissible to ask a question?"

Straight-faced, I responded, "You just did." The hand fell as if its 'string' were suddenly cut. The course had begun.

The Training Group (T-Group) model I was employing radically reconfigured traditional classroom protocol. With this new model, what I came to call Peer-Group Learning, the teacher demurred from active leadership responsibilities in the classroom, precipitating an inversion of the usual teacher-student roles.

As I well knew, such an approach to teaching was not for the faint of heart. Typically, the hapless teacher would eventually be – almost literally – killed off by rebellious students assuming responsibility for their own learning. Though many students flourished under this model, others, as I soon discovered, faded. These latter students concluded, "If the teacher isn't going to do anything, why should I?"

As evidenced in two papers I published during this period,[3] I was at least intellectually aware of the problems inherent in Peer-Group Learning:

> *By way of scholarly defense, I have tried to make a sustained logical argument ... for the necessity of Peer-Group Learning.... But, as in the case of all logical arguments, once put into practice, compromise is inevitable. In practical experience, there is absolutely no room for dogmatism.*

As "absolutely no room" indicates, I was comically caught in the paradoxical position of arguing dogmatically against dogmatism. Setting out to free the educational system from dogmatism, I had succeeded only in promoting and perpetuating a dogmatism of my own making.

Like charity, criticism best begins at home. To guard against dogmatic literalism in our experience, we must begin by confronting the literalism embedded in our own thinking. In attempting to do so, here are some questions we have found useful to consider:

- Does our literal interpretation bring us into conflict with others? Does it cause us to exclude them, however subtly, from the circle of humanity?

- Are we clinging so tightly to cherished forms from the past or imagined forms for the future that we prevent our hopes and ideals from manifesting in unexpected, or yet unimagined, ways?

---

3   See "Learning Without Authority" in *The Religious Situation: 1969*, edited by Donald Cutler, Beacon Press, 1969; Randall Huntsberry and Myron Glazer, "Just What Is a Teacher, Anyway?" in *Educational Therapy*, edited by Marshall B. Rosenberg, Bernie Straub Publishing Co., 1973.

- What role does fear play in our rigid adherence to a form? Does that fear serve a useful purpose?

- Is strict adherence to a form our way of precluding fear, rather than dealing with the thing feared? If so, what long-range impact does this denial have on our lives?

- Can we remain flexible while simultaneously maintaining our stability? Can we let go of fear and allow new forms to evolve that still faithfully embody the essence of what we hold sacred or essential in our lives?

Literalism, fundamentalism, and dogmatism reinforce one another. In an increasingly transient society, we must all find ways to preserve what we most value from the past and simultaneously remain open to change. This combination of flexibility and stability is an essential survival skill in any venue.

Our richly multicultural and rapidly changing world requires a mental state of equilibrium when encountering differences with others or in the face of the new or unexpected. To realize this openness, it is important that we not equate difference with danger or change with loss.

We have the right to our own beliefs and to the choice of our path in life. But regardless of the earnestness of our intent and the certainty of our convictions, we are not always doing what we think we are doing. It is all too easy to be self-deceived. Perhaps the 'way' is less a question of this road or that than of listening as we go.

SANCTUARY

There is no peace of heart
if we don't put the sky inside.

~ Anonymous

In a time when, day in and day out, airwaves scream with the politics of fear, we are all increasingly at risk of becoming victimized by what President Franklin D. Roosevelt called the fear of "fear itself."

Regardless of our physical or social circumstances, none of us is truly free without freedom from fear. But often in today's political climate, there seems to be no sanctuary, no place to hide from the assault of fear on individual consciousness.

One meaning of the word 'sanctuary' is a place of refuge, a protected oasis affording asylum, immunity. For wildlife, it defines a safe place, sheltered from hunters and trappers, where birds and animals can procreate and raise their young. For either man or beast, sanctuary represents a space free of fear.

Any form of creative endeavor requires a similar kind of space – a mental sanctuary. When creativity or problem solving are called for, even if outward circumstances are unthreatening, we may find ourselves assailed by anxious or fearful thoughts, distracting us from the vital practice of listening.

When we are afraid, we feel robbed of control, even the control of our own thought processes, and this usually leads to feeling victimized. One distinctive characteristic of this 'victim mentality' is a sense of powerlessness in the face of danger.

Another trait of victimization, more subtle perhaps, is that of self-centered-ness. Thought circles around with self-concern, repeating over and over a feeling of helplessness. For all its appearance of agitated, even frenetic activity, this endless spinning hypnotizes our mentalities and ultimately generates nothing.

Yet, no matter how helpless we feel when afraid, we do have the power to break free of this self-centered circling and reclaim control of our thinking.

The most direct way out of fear's victimization is to make our first priority the sanctity of our inner mental space. In order to create and preserve that sanctuary, we must watch the suggestions that come into consciousness and learn to say "yes" and "no" – "yes" to listening and "no" to fear.

YES AND NO

But let your communication be,
Yea, yea; Nay, nay ...

~ Saint Matthew

Every motor vehicle requires at least two control mechanisms, an accelera-tor and a brake. The same is true of our own mentalities.

Suppose we have only a brake pedal. Our thought processes may roll for-ward on inertia, but our single power to act is to retard or stop the motion; we have no ability to impel it forward. Limited to "no," we may find our-selves acting as perpetual 'nay-sayers.' On any creative project, we can all too easily kill the creative impulse with negativity almost before it gets underway.

We may not habitually take this role, but most of us have expressed or encountered a nay-sayer mentality from time to time. On the other hand, we may have experienced in someone – ourselves or another – a tendency to ride the opposite pedal.

If we are equipped only with an accelerator, we can start up our thought processes easily enough. But without a brake, we may be tempted under pressure to jam down all the harder on the pedal we do have – the gas. Without the ability to slow down and consider our alternatives, or to stop the direction of our thoughts and change course, we may overshoot this and bang into that until, frustrated, angry, and exhausted, we crash.

To maximize our creative potential, both pedals are required. With experience and practice, we must learn to exercise the discipline of saying "yes" to thoughts that would further our creative processes and "no" to those that would sabotage us with fear.

*Chery: Both Ran and I find our workshops with **Listening Unlimited** deeply enjoyable. But whereas Ran usually approaches these events with a relaxed, easygoing attitude, I tend to define our responsibilities in detail, and then monitor them every step of the way.*

In the past, this concern has affected my ability during a workshop to sleep at night. As much as I tried, I could not seem to turn off the 'fear-static' and rest. Eventually, especially by the end of a six-day workshop, exhaustion would compromise my joy and (poor Ran can attest, as he usually suffered the brunt of it) my sweet temper.

Some time ago, directly before a weeklong workshop we were leading, I announced to Ran that I was determined not to become taxed with worry and depleted. No matter what happened, I would not allow myself to feel victimized by circumstances I could not control. I would control what I could control – my own thoughts – and maintain the inner peace necessary to listen.

A full week before we arrived on campus, I met my first test. Two students' pre-workshop papers were late, preventing me from emailing the complete packet of papers to all workshop participants.

One of the remiss students sent me an email, but forgot to attach his paper, and then danced off, satisfied his obligations were dispatched. The other failed to respond at all, despite repeated pleas. I later learned I had sent these pleas to a defunct email address. After a couple of days, I received the first of the missing papers and made the decision then to send the incomplete packet off to everyone.

Normally, in a case like this, I would have become agitated, concerned that one or two participants were imposing upon all the rest, and uncertain at what point I should accept a compromise and send the papers out piecemeal. But with this workshop, I had resolved to remain still and listen.

In attempting to keep this resolution, I found myself passing through several mental steps. Looking back, I realize that these steps were what allowed me to say "no" or "yes" to each thought – fearful or otherwise – that came to mind. The four steps were as follows:

1. *Simply **recognize** that I felt victimized.*

2. *Treat any fear I experience merely as an **alert**, a reminder to listen, not as a power able to take away my peace.*

3. ***Reject** the resentful, put-upon mindset of a victim and **assert** my right to maintain my inner sanctuary.*

4. *Get down to my proper business – **listening**.*

In retrospect, the concerns involved here seem minuscule. But for me, this incident constituted a major turning point in my arrival at a more consistent practice of creative listening. And it prepared me for the week to come.

During the workshop, a number of challenges naturally surfaced. Each time, I put my four steps to work. In every instance, solutions unfolded which perfectly met our needs and, more often than not, without my having to do anything but govern my own thinking.

Of course, it was gratifying for me to watch these solutions appear. But even more important, it was edifying to witness every challenge transform from a stumbling block into a stepping stone, a celebrative opportunity to exercise my autonomy over fear.

As proof of success, I fell asleep easily at the end of each day for the first time ever, and – without struggle – I maintained my equilibrium and joy throughout the workshop. Since that time, I have been able to apply this same practice successfully in many other instances, large and small.

Our first priority when encountering fear is *not to lose ourselves*. Not to lose our listening center. Maintaining that mental sanctuary is what protects us from becoming fear's puppet, its victim. By monitoring our thoughts, we can choose which ones to entertain, when to apply the accelerator and when to apply the brake.

VICTIMIZATION VS. SOVEREIGNTY

*Do you think
or just think you think?*

~ John H. Wyndham

With the practice of improvisation, as with life in general, we are not as a rule granted the power to control other people's choices or actions. Yet, although fear-based thoughts seem to claim otherwise, we do have the ability to control our own.

Our primary task in claiming self-control is to choose what role we want to play and stick to it. Why should we allow fear to make us into something we do not want to be?

Whatever our outward circumstances, they alone cannot make us a victim. The role of victim is ultimately an inner, mental one. And we have sovereign power to refuse that role in relation to any person or circumstance no matter how severe a situation or grave an offence we have suffered.

We can assert and demonstrate our sovereignty by taking responsibility for how we respond to the thoughts that come to us. To do this, we must resist the temptation to ruminate. Instead of allowing our minds to become enslaved by anger and hurt, incessantly reiterating our grievance and blaming others, we can choose the direction of our own attention.

Ran: The occasion of my tenure denial at Wesleyan was, up to that point in my life, the greatest affront I had ever faced. The temptation to blame the faculty for their shortsightedness was immense.

Fortunately, there were strong indications of a negative outcome far in advance. This lag allowed me time to accept the fact that opposition to my case was a predictable pushback from a system I had challenged all along.

I had been a rebellious junior faculty, upsetting colleagues with my dress, my way of teaching, my refusal to play by the rules. Upon reflection, I realized this was an angry reaction to my own educational experience, and this anger signaled that fear was in the driver's seat.

I still believed in educational reform, but I had to admit that my tactics had been inappropriate, as well as ineffectual. Pressing the peddle to the metal, I had attempted to move a structure far weightier than my little vehicle could budge.

By the time the tenure vote was taken, I was thoroughly at peace with the situation and blamed no one but myself. I could take every anticipated negative vote and trace it back to my own behavior.

Too late to rectify the situation at Wesleyan, I finally grasped the fact that the secret to learning I had sought to introduce into my classrooms, I had failed to practice with my colleagues – the profound importance of listening.

Over the past thirty years, I have put this hard-won insight to good use, counseling others caught up in similar situations. I have found special pleasure in watching their self-destructive behaviors fall away, and creative freedom emerge.

However justified a reaction of anger – or mere annoyance – may seem, it is likely rooted in fear. And we have a right to defend our consciousness against fear's affliction. Controlling our reactions, refusing to become distracted or consumed by fear and its offshoots, demands that we focus instead on our own creative direction and growth.

If we pass through a rough experience and grow thereby, why should we spend our time ruminating, victimized by anger? Inadvertently, our adversary – or perhaps it is just a challenging situation – has impelled us to practice our ability to listen and grow. Why should we not be grateful for the lessons, however hard won, and move on?

Nursing anger harms us, because it binds us to its source: fear. "[A]nd fear hath torment," as Saint John avers. Conversely, letting go of anger and its various manifestations – resentment, irritation, self-justification, or hurt – reestablishes our sovereign control over our own mentality and restores our peace. In the deepest sense, we create our own worlds, and then live in them.

HUMILITY

We study the self
to forget the self.

~ Zen saying

Often such an approach to adversity requires that we adopt an attitude of humility rather than one of humiliation. These two terms, though from the same root word, imply virtually opposite mental states.

'Humiliation' signifies the presence of pride and self-importance, whereas 'humility' expresses a receptivity, elasticity, and gentleness that indicate the absence of conceit. With humiliation, self is front and center. With humility, the discoveries made and lessons learned take center stage.

The classic example of humility vs. humiliation is the willow and the oak. The willow bends under the battering storm, then returns unharmed to its upright position after the winds have passed. The oak, remaining unreceptive and rigid, cracks under the force of the winds. With humility, we learn from our circumstances and move on. With humiliation, we are broken by them.

SELF-DETERMINATION

*That which is not honored
can become perverse.*

~ Anonymous

Chery: *I remember reading an article years ago, describing a scientific study on identical twins. To my best recollection, the purpose of the study was to explore how nurture affects personality development.*

One set of twin brothers, raised in a home with an alcoholic father, still resided in the town where they grew up. One of the twins had followed in his father's footsteps, gaining the reputation of a ne'er-do-well and town drunk. The study described this man as bitter and resentful, unable to hold down a job or maintain a committed relationship.

By contrast, the study found his brother quiet and modest. Highly regarded in the community, this brother was recognized as a successful businessman, an important church and community volunteer, and a devoted husband and father.

When interviewed, each man was asked the same question: to what do you attribute the course of your life?

The first brother replied, "Look at my father. What else could I have become?" His identical twin answered, "Look at my father. What else could I have become?"

We may feel many things that happen in our lives are beyond our control, but how we respond to and what we take away from these circumstances are not. When an experience has been hurtful, even deeply unjust, how we respond is our choice. We can choose victimization or self-determination.

As Chery's mother advised her early on, "Identify what is most challenging in your life. Reverse it. And you will find your calling." In other words, instead of mindlessly reacting to adversity as did the first twin, we can *listen* to its lessons. And like his brother, what we learn becomes our strength, our perfect compensation, our recompense.

In improvisation, this same principle applies. Not what happens, but what a dancer does with what happens is the determining factor in a performance. Every event, no matter what its nature, if embraced and incorporated, expands, deepens, and enriches the dance.

The secret lies in where the attention of the dancer is placed. In the process of its performance, an improvisation is not about the dancer. It is about the dance. When a performer's attention is sidetracked to personal concerns of anxiety or affront, the dance suffers.

Such concerns cannot of themselves impede the progress of the dance. Properly viewed, they only provide further grist for the mill of creativity. And the same is true of our lives.

Our ability to listen unleashes our creative potential. Allowing ourselves to indulge in a sense of victimization blocks that listening. To make the choice to listen in the face of anger or fear may require at times deep reflection and persistent resolve, but it is well worth the effort. More than any one thing, it determines our autonomy.

MOVEMENT MEDITATION

There are more things possible
than people think.

~ John Locke

Improvisers often remark on the sense of ease and peace they experience with the practice of the improvisational mind. Sometimes we are asked if we see what we are teaching in our workshops as 'movement meditation.'

We do recognize creative listening as a kind of meditation, but not in the technical sense of the word. The purpose behind our 'meditative' practice is to generate the best possible improvisations and interactions.

To be able to improvise optimally, we first establish a listening focus within ourselves. Then, maintaining this meditative centeredness, we expand our awareness to interact with others and the environment.

This practice enables us to open our awareness to the influences of others and the environment without losing touch with ourselves. And likewise, it allows us to hear our own inner voice without blocking out the voices around us.

In daily life-practice as well, we all need to find mental sanctuary. Sometimes we have periods or places of quiet and solitude in which to access it. At other times, we are forced to seek sanctuary in the very midst of life's commotion.

Unlike physical sanctuaries, our mental sanctuary is not an outward circumstance, but an inward state of listening with which we approach our activities and interactions. Creativity, crisis management, and human relationships are all daily improvisational opportunities that call for mental sanctuary from fear.

Ran: Having a mental sanctuary has always been important to me. I can still remember how difficult it was to share a tiny bedroom with my younger siblings. I had no space in which to collect myself.

In the corner of our room, I kept an orange crate where I stashed everything I valued. This crate was all I had of physical sanctuary. Obviously, it was just a symbol. What little true sanctuary I could find was what I bore in my mind.

Since that time, I have always struggled to support my mental sanctuary by preserving my private physical space. An illustration of this arose during an around-the-world tour, when I served with seven other faculty as chaperone to a diverse group of graduate students from twenty-six countries and twelve religions.

Before we embarked, I insisted upon having a room of my own booked at each location where I could retreat, usually very late at night, to listen to myself, work on a poem, or just relax. During the tour, several crises points occurred when the sanctuary of my room helped me maintain my mental balance.

Once, in Egypt, a faculty contingent informed me that they wanted to send the 'political troublemakers' in the student group home when the rest of us left for Rome. Since my colleagues had excluded me from their preliminary deliberations, I felt they must have doubted whether I would support their plan.

In any case, I excused myself, retreated to my sanctuary, and listened. In that quiet space, it became clear to me that sending this small contingent home would undermine the morale of the remaining one hundred thirty students, and that the tour from that point on would inevitably deteriorate, possibly collapse.

Besides, I reasoned, the disruption that these rebels caused was relatively minor. I had suffered far worse troublemakers in my time.

I shared these thoughts with my colleagues. After brief consideration, they decided to back off. We proceeded with the tour as originally planned, and soon enough, the students settled down.

Those labeled 'troublemakers,' of course, were the natural leaders of the group. At the end of the tour, I felt particularly gratified when these same students organized a talent show for our final banquet. The theme of the show, satirizing all of the internal battles we had weathered together, left everyone roaring with laughter, happily bonded, and wholly satisfied.

The sanctuary found in listening without fear centers and balances us, placing us at the helm of our own thoughts. Establishing such a sanctuary demands discipline, especially in our modern age with its onslaught of sensational images vying for our attention, indeed our minds. But the consistent practice of creative listening promises nothing less than what all deep mental or spiritual practice promises – a transformative adventure.

PART THREE

LEADERSHIP

At the highest level,
the work of a leader is to lead conversations
about what's essential and what's not.

~ Ronald Heifetz

All too often leadership is associated with fear. For those in subordinate positions, it is typically the fear of domination; for those in leadership positions, the fear of insubordination.

Fear constricts interpersonal communication and undermines teamwork. Mutual respect, on the other hand, enables both parties in an interaction, even under pressure, to continue listening receptively to one another.

Respect of subordinates for their leaders and vice versa is a necessary element of any hierarchical power structure. It supports professional cooperation. Respect, however, does not flow from hierarchal authority *per se*. It has to be won.

True leadership begins with picking up on the right idea at the right time, and this can only be accomplished through listening. In touch with what is most salient in any given circumstance, such leadership – whether exhibited by a 'leader' or a 'subordinate' – demonstrates authority.

LEADERSHIP THROUGH DOMINATION

A great man shows his greatness
by the way he treats little men.

~ Thomas Carlyle

Unfortunately, people in all walks of life too frequently believe that having a *position* of authority gives them the right to lead not by listening, but by fear. Who among us has not, at one time or another, had bosses or colleagues or even subordinates who attempted to get their way by bullying those around them?

Because many of us shy away from conflict, or are afraid of the social or professional consequences of standing up to authority, we all too often 'go along to get along,' and the bully in our lives goes unchallenged.

Ran: Not long ago, I had occasion to visit with a former client, a departmental manager of a mid-sized company. I had always been impressed by [Madeline's] work ethic and positive attitude, and I considered her a model employee. So I was completely taken aback to learn she had just been fired. What could possibly have precipitated this action?

Madeline described her boss as a retired career military officer who intimidated even the owner of the company. Instead of consulting with associates, he barked orders. In staff meetings, he made cutting personal remarks if anyone so much as appeared to challenge his point of view.

In one such meeting, after suffering his repeated derision, Madeline finally lost it and shouted, "You are not my father!" Immediately regretting her outburst, she knew she was in for it.

"Right! I'm not your father," he yelled back, "but I am your boss!" The next day, he fired her.

Although Madeline has left the company, her former colleagues keep her informed. Morale has hit rock bottom, and people are finding devious ways to act out their anger. Unable to confront their bully-boss directly without risking their jobs, they are simply failing to provide the functional support he needs to do his.

Chickens, it seems, have a way of coming home to roost.

Fear does not generate motivated workers. If intimidated, employees or colleagues will often 'go along,' but only in a desultory way.

When leaders fail to win employee 'buy-in,' not only do they lose the opportunity to tap the creative energies of their employees, but over time, the company as a whole suffers from poor quality work and high turnover costs.

LEADERSHIP THROUGH LISTENING

The greatest expert ... is the one
who can listen.

~ Glen Lauder

In 1970, Robert K. Greenleaf published his groundbreaking essay, *The Servant as Leader*.[1] Here he identifies ten critical characteristics of the 'servant-leader,' the first of which is listening.[2]

According to Greenleaf, a true leader does not sit at the apex of the managerial pyramid dispatching orders. Greenleaf believes lasting power comes from the bottom up, turning the traditional pyramid on its head.

The 'listening model' he espouses is a team model. Its working assumption: the wisdom of a team is greater than the wisdom of any individual member. But this theory holds true only if everyone listens to everyone else, and with especial attention to individuals who appear to have nothing to say.

Unless a team nourishes such a culture, its operations will be dominated by the solitary wisdom of the member with the most authority or the most muscle.

In Greenleaf's model, the leader's role is not to manage and control other people, but to help them manage and control themselves. *Listening*, not the person in charge, is the source of power.

---

1   Robert K. Greenleaf, *The Servant as Leader*, Indianapolis, Indiana: Robert K. Greenleaf Center for Servant-Leadership, 1970, 1991.

2   Ran reflects further on this counter-intuitive approach to leadership in his book, *Listening Out Loud: The Leadership Paradox*, New York: iUniversity Press, 2001.

By listening attentively to each player, the servant-leader excavates the wisdom of the entire team, helping the group and its individual members achieve their personal and shared goals. Aiding and encouraging team-mates to develop their talents, a leader can create a 'win-win' situation for the collective and its members alike.

TOP-DOWN AND BOTTOM-UP

There are two types of people –
those who come into a room and say,
"Well, here I am!"
and those who come in and say,
"Ah, there you are!"

~ Fredrich L. Collins

In 2004, the American Olympic Basketball Team failed to bring home the gold. Some sports reporters pointed out that a collection of the highest paid stars in the NBA does not in itself produce the best team. As the say-ing goes, the name on the front of the jersey is what matters, not the name on the back.

Ran: From an early age, I understood the necessity of teamwork in sports. But the team leadership I knew was always 'top-down.' And in every sport I ever played, there was a domineering coach pushing the players along.

In high school, I attempted to lead several organizations the way I assumed leaders were supposed to lead. As state Lieutenant Governor of Key Club International, for instance, I used my muscle to force the selection of the next Key Club Governor at the state convention.

When it came to brains, my candidate was indisputably the best qualified. But, as I was about to learn, brains were not all that counted. What mattered more were the social skills he lacked to make him the popular choice. With my endorsement, he won the election, but without a loyal following, his term as Governor proved a disaster.

My experiments with top-down management eventually took their toll on me personally. Exhausted by the stress, I vowed that in college I would avoid leadership positions altogether.

In my freshman year, knowing it involved no managerial duties, I volunteered as a wrestling coach at a nearby Cambridge settlement house. By the end of term, I had come to love everything about this experience, especially my one-on-one contact with the kids.

The following year, I was asked to manage all of the Harvard volunteers in my settlement house. At first, I thought I could do this in addition to coaching. But once again, over-commitment got the best of me, and I had to let the coaching go.

The next year, I was recruited to manage all Harvard settlement house volunteers in the Boston area. The responsibility was daunting. I hardly knew where to begin.

Following my father's suggestion, I constructed a four-tier managerial grid with a multi-boxed diagram of descending authority. It was a thing of beauty ... but became, as Max Weber[3] concluded of all bureaucracy, my 'iron cage.' Not only was this top-down system stressful, it removed me even further from the children I so enjoyed. I soldiered on, but I was miserable.

At the end of my junior year, I was asked to oversee all Harvard volunteer programs. This time I bowed out. Lesson learned. I have since rarely assumed a top position in any organization. Instead, I coach the bosses.

After graduation, a 'bottom-up' leadership style became the foundation of Ran's approach to teaching, counseling, and eventually corporate coaching. In all these roles, questions of leadership and power – and their relation to listening – perennially arose.

---

3   Max Weber, *The Protestant Ethic and the Spirit of Capitalism,* translated by Talcott Parsons, London: Routledge, 2001.

If listening and teamwork are so effective, he wondered, why do so many leaders choose to motivate their subordinates through fear? The answer he came to is proverbial: leaders who govern by fear are governed by fear.

Underneath it all, the fear leaders face is one of failure. At the very least, they dread embarrassment, diminished authority, or loss of control.

What results when fear drives a leader? At best, micromanaging, at worst, bullying. The only way to break this cycle is to find the courage – and it does take courage – to let go of the need to *personally* control the over-all situation and everyone in it, and instead, seek out ways to facilitate employees' greater self-management.

In a world of uncertainty and impermanence, any individual's attempt at omnipotent control is doomed to failure. If a leader does not find a way to build mutually respectful and trusting relationships with associates, he or she is destined to fall short of the highest possible success and, doubtless, to inflict upon him or herself some form of hurt.

LISTENING AND POWER

As we are liberated from our own fear,
our presence automatically
liberates others.

~ Nelson Mandela

The connection of leadership to listening and listening to power is not uni-versally accepted. In fact, in the minds of many, listening and power are considered opposites.

Some may interpret listening as a copout, the passive stance of someone too weak or insecure to speak up. Others may suspiciously regard it as a crafty tactic, a cover for gathering ammunition in a debate or dispute, with the intent to manipulate others rather than to communicate with or understand them.

Of course, listening can be used to hide out or to manipulate. But we contend that these forms of listening lack the three-dimensional balance of attention to self, other, and environment that constitutes creative listening.

They fall into a category we call *selective listening*. Selective listening is listening with an agenda, that is, with an intention other than to accurately understand, for the benefit of all, what is going on.

To our way of thinking, selective listening results from fear, which at some level, arises from a sense of powerlessness. In this crucial aspect, selective listening fundamentally diverges from creative listening.

So how do we distinguish listening as power from listening as weakness? Here are three criteria:

- Listening is power when it leads to action, even if at times that 'action' is the free choice to remain still or silent.

- Listening is power when its focus of attention is three-dimensional, not just selective.

- And finally, listening is power when motivated by interest or respect, not fear.

Chery: In my Wesleyan course, Dance Teaching Workshop: Theory and Practice, *one assignment always proved a favorite. Every student-teacher was to prepare a short movement activity. In class, he or she presented this activity twice, in each case playing a different caricature of a teacher. The first caricature was meek and timid, the second, tyrannical.*

The result was unfailingly comical. Other members of the class, participating as 'students,' fought heroically to maintain their composure, stifling almost irrepressible laughter as they followed the directions of these teacher-clowns.

Interestingly enough, the class always found the whole exercise vaguely – sometimes vividly – familiar. Most had experienced teachers at one time or another of both ilks.

For young, first-time dance teachers, finding an optimal balance between permissiveness and strict control was almost a moral struggle. Few were comfortable with either extreme. But everyone agreed that each extremity had its advantage and disadvantage.

When the teacher was non-assertive, the students tended to take control of the class. They enjoyed the freedom to be creative, to find and express their own ideas. But scattered in multiple directions, their energies and attention dissipated, and eventually anarchy reigned.

When the teacher was tyrannical, the class proceeded in a more focused, orderly manner. Material was conveyed efficiently from teacher to student. The downside was that the students were never encouraged to initiate anything, and certainly not to think for themselves.

As a part of the course practicum, each student-teacher taught a mini-course of his or her own. Here they often confronted the necessity of assuming roles foreign to their self-images.

A student-teacher who loved open dialogue might face a class unprepared for freedom and desperately in need of direction. A teacher who preferred dictating every detail might find his or her class unchallenged by this approach, sitting back in a dazed lethargy and letting their teacher do all the work.

As my students inevitably concluded, leadership was as much about listening and following as it was about planning and directing. It required as much responsiveness and adaptability as it did initiative and vision.

No matter how 'take charge' or 'laid back' a teacher's classroom persona, they decided, good leaders had to be good followers.

The 'listening model' of leadership is not for the uncourageous or self-serving. To be successful, it cannot be assumed partially or dishonestly. Selective listening is not a legitimate cover for a leader too insecure to take a stand. Success is equally compromised when the intent is to manipulate rather than reveal.

If fully employed, however, the listening model can be highly effective. There is a remarkable power in listening with the three-dimensional intention of understanding our own needs, the needs and concerns of others, and the realities of our environment. Indeed, such listening has the potential to harness the wisdom and creative resources of an entire community.

EDUCATION

If you teach a man anything
he will never learn.

~ George Bernard Shaw

The freedom to fail is what makes learning possible. No new territory is blazed without it. The trial and error of experimentation, so essential to creativity, is at the very heart of learning.

Education at its finest is a feast of discovery. And for us, learning how to tap our creativity is the *piece de resistance* of the educational process, not an incidental side dish or decorative garnish.

In this age of electronics and computers, information is relatively easy to obtain. In fact, we are bombarded by it. But information alone is unable to engender the ability to think or act creatively.

Traditional learning, with its emphasis on the transmission of information and general theory, does not necessarily come with the good judgment to use this information wisely, the ability to apply it creatively, or the qualities of character necessary to put it successfully into practice.

Along with knowledge of our past and present world, how then, do we develop wisdom, creativity, and confidence? We know of only two ways: through listening and examined experience.

Until now, our discussion has focused on the first point, listening. So let us take a moment here to address the second, experience.

EXPERIENTIAL EDUCATION

I hear and I forget,
I see and I remember,
I do and I understand.

~ Aikido saying

Experiential education is messy and expensive. It takes space, time, and daring. But the demands it makes upon students can reveal to them the stuff of which they are made. Consequently, learning through experience is often especially memorable, even profoundly so.

Naturally, it is much easier to have one authority figure at the head of the class lecturing, with everyone else taking notes. Upon graduating, however, most of us quickly discover that all those facts, stored away so conscientiously in our notebooks, fade from memory with amazing speed.

In the long run, an education comprised of nothing but second-hand learning has serious limitations. This is not to say that reflection and analysis have no place. Indeed, they are fundamental. They provide information and perspective, and they develop a student's reasoning and critical capacities.

But facts and logic alone do not prepare us adequately to make the important decisions of our lives. Thinking and talking *about* life are light-years away from living it, and even further from living it creatively.

Of course, the teaching of creativity costs money, and part of the problem in advancing this kind of education is limited resources. It is understandable why administrators tend to fall back on a vision of education emphasizing the passing on of traditional learning, and sacrifice programs cultivating creativity. It simply costs less. But obviously, anytime finances take precedence over educational purpose, the entire enterprise is at risk.

Theory without practice is like clouds without rain. Yet unfortunately, when the bottom line becomes money instead of educational vision, experiential programs that introduce practice – whether laboratory courses, athletics, or the arts – go on the block.

TRADITION AND CHANGE

Don't worry about people stealing your ideas.
If your ideas are any good,
you'll have to ram them down people's throats.

~ Howard Aiken

Chery: *My dance colleagues and I saw the Dance Department as a meeting of two traditions: professional dance and academia. Neither scholarship nor technical training was seen as an end in itself. Both were subordinated to cultivating the creative thinker, a goal shared by artist and scholar alike.*

By making creativity its keystone, the department embraced equally the academic and artistic traditions, expanding its curricular approach to include reflection and analysis, without losing commitment to performative excellence.

During numerous departmental reviews, many Wesleyan opponents of the dance program came to appreciate the value of dance and its place in the university. Not long after each review was completed, however, the thinking of these new supporters would often revert to the ingrained and familiar, and they would end up back in their old neighborhoods of thought.

Habits die hard. To break cycles of recidivism requires dedicated and steadfast resolve. Sometimes, for generations.

Even within the world of market-driven corporate training, Ran experienced this same tendency to cling to the past.

Ran: *During an Interpersonal Communications Workshop (ICW), [Anthony], a bluntly outspoken engineer, gained sudden insight into why his behavior so often provoked collegial hostility. He determined then and there to change.*

Some years later at a follow-up workshop, I had occasion to meet Anthony again. I remembered his 'conversion' experience and asked him how his 'reform' had gone.

"In the beginning, not all that well," he responded sheepishly. "In fact, on my first day back at work, a colleague, who seemed quite agitated for no reason I could see, cornered me and asked what was wrong. He said that I had been acting really weird all day, starting with the morning staff meeting.

*"I explained that I had recently been to 'charm school' and had seen what an S.O.B. I had been all these years. And, I added, I was determined to change. At this point, my colleague exploded, 'Tony, you may be an S.O.B., but you are **my** S.O.B.!'"*

It appears that Anthony's colleague was struggling with the change required of *him* by Anthony's reform. As bad as it was, living with the familiar was just easier.

Real change is difficult, even scary. Old habits and routines make change and the acceptance of change problematic in any venue.

Expanding experiential learning within traditional academia necessarily involves change. Sadly for students, educators too often find it not only easier, but safer, to block curricular innovation.

'STEPPING OUT OF THE BOX'

People who tell the truth
should keep their horse saddled.

~ Caucasus proverb

Everyone knows that to watch from the sidelines is infinitely easier than to actually do something – anything. Experiential learning is not the easy way out. It demands that we put ourselves on the line, that we get off our mental backsides and act.

First-hand experience encourages students to think for themselves, which fosters conviction and authority. Because experience gives students a foundation upon which to come to their own conclusions, it also invites them to 'step out of the box.'

The result is a person who is harder to control. For this reason alone, it should not be surprising that institutions, whose day-to-day business is to maintain stability, so often resist an experiential approach to learning.

Process and Product

What we learn with pleasure
we never forget.

~ Louis Mercier

How might we begin to reverse this resistance to experiential learning? One way is to ask, "What should our process be, if our product is learning? Is there a consistency between our means and our ends?"

In our opinion, too often the emphasis falls on the end product, grades and test scores, rather than on the learning process itself, the ability to think and create. Here dance may provide a simple but thought-provoking analogy.

What if we focused only on the conclusion of a dance instead of attending its process? We would miss the dance altogether. The experience of life itself is very much the same; the end is not really the point.

One may counter that the performing arts are possibly freer to celebrate the value of process than are other disciplines, in part because there exists no universally accepted scorecard for its product, for artistic excellence. But art is not the only venue in which focusing on process, not just product, is vital. Process is just as critical in competitive sports, where a scorecard certainly does exist.

Chery: Walter, my financial advisor, has spent countless hours coaching little league baseball. Although highly competitive himself, the child is his main focus, not winning the game. But even in the business of winning, he avows, the process and its enjoyment are the true keys to success.

From his experience as a coach, Walter tells the following story: "One year, I had a terrific player. But in the heat of a game with two strikes on him, he tended to take a called strike three. He clutched.

"'If you're going down,' I told him, 'go down swinging. When you've got two strikes on you, be daring. Make hard contact with a good level swing. Go for it!

"'And if you miss, that's OK. Every great player misses sometimes. The important thing is how you react afterwards.'

"I worked with this kid several months," Walter continues. "It didn't happen overnight. In fact, one afternoon at a game, I could see him seizing up once again. I went over to him. 'Don't try to win this game all by yourself,' I said. 'Just try to execute what we've been practicing. Just make solid contact with the ball.'

"Well, he hit a double into left center, and we could see his Cheshire Cat grin all the way from behind home plate!"

What Walter teaches is process, how to face and conquer fear, first by simplifying the issues and then by focusing affirmatively on the immediate task at hand. Like Walter, we adhere to the conviction that in education, process is more important than product, because the highest goal of education is learning how to learn.

At the end of the day, this kind of education is what produces excellence not only in process, but also in product. And it is the kind of learning we never forget.

The Ephemeral and the Enduring

Beautiful things …
always carry greetings from other worlds
within them.

~ Elaine Scary

Because our life experiences share so many qualities in common with dance, and especially with movement improvisation, we have found the study of both dance and improvisation inimitably suited to education.

One commonality improvisation and human life share is their ephemerality. Both bloom in splendor, only to pass away.

Movement improvisers, when improvising well, feel keenly alive and engaged. One essential reason the experience is so vivid is that it requires all aspects of consciousness – kinetic, emotional, intellectual, even spiritual – and because it often calls upon depths of courage and character.

But when the dance is over, what is left? Just a fleeting rush that quickly fades? Not necessarily.

When a model of education is employed where *reflection* is brought to bear upon *action*, something of enduring value remains after the immediate event is over. The thoughts or ideas gleaned from this experience are like seeds gathered from a flower past its bloom. They can be planted in another time or place to blossom again.

With this educational model, individuals perform a dance and, either during the dance or afterwards, consciously reflect upon their actions. Through this action/reflection process, they gain insight and understanding, culling from a single ephemeral experience, perceptions applicable in other venues.

In the process of gathering and sowing, repeated *ad infinitum*, the ephemeral gains its own kind of immortality.

Chery: When at Wesleyan, I taught a dance history course entitled May I Have the Pleasure. *It explored the interface between social dance forms and the overarching social, political, and religious structures and values of the Renaissance, Baroque, and early 19ᵗʰ century periods in European history.*

Students learned to perform dances from each period, viewed films portraying the times, and read historical commentary. 'Stepping into the shoes' of people from another time seemed to have a peculiarly revelatory effect, bringing history alive in an almost visceral way. Like actors donning corsets from a bygone era, students 'felt' something of the mentality of the times.

It was not an easy task for beginning dancers to learn what courtiers once spent hours a day perfecting. In order to convey a real sense of these dances, I had to find ways to move my students from a mechanical grasp of the steps to a more kinetic feel and mastery.

In teaching the waltz, for instance, one of the techniques I used was to plunge dancers unexpectedly into total darkness for a few moments, taking away their ability to rely on vision for orientation.

Without visual cues, partners were forced to depend entirely on listening aurally to the music and kinetically to one another. In a crowded studio, they had also to sense the proximity of the other couples dancing around them.

Students reported with surprise that in the pitch-blackness they suddenly became more graceful, feeling the movement, rather than thinking it. And remarkably, they were far less likely to bump into those around them when sightless. Unable to direct their steps visually, they were forced to listen.

One day, I was speaking with a student in this course who declared enthusiastically, "My favorite part of the whole class is waltzing in the dark."

"Why is that, exactly?" I asked him. I had heard this from students before.

"I don't know," Jon shrugged dismissively.

I waited. With a look of deepening reflection, he continued, "Well, whatever it is ... it's something neither of my parents had in any of their marriages."

"And what is that?"

"I don't know," Jon replied. But I could see him listening inwardly now to recapture that kinetic experience.

Then, with a revelatory smile, he exclaimed, "Trust!"

Dance is ephemeral, but when reflected upon, can yield lasting insight. The wisdom to be gained through experiential learning addresses all dimensions of human consciousness – physical, emotional, intellectual, spiritual. In so doing, it places a mirror before our very lives.

INTIMACY

There is no fear in love;
but perfect love casteth out fear.

~ Saint Paul

Listening creates a state of intimacy with everything around us. As with partners in a waltz, the practice of listening tends to bring us into natural accord with the movement of others and of life's events, sometimes in moments of synchronicity so stunning, they leave us awestruck.

Fear does just the opposite. To the degree that we feel frightened, our listening becomes impaired, and we lose the intimate state, the connecting rod of the improvisational mind.

CREATING INTIMACY

Where can I find a man
who has forgotten words?
I would like to have a word with him.

~ Chuang Tzu

Intimacy is dependent not on the presence of another person, but upon the presence of listening. It is created by our own attention to and respect for whatever and whomever is at hand.

Ran: At one point during the years I taught at Wesleyan, I attended a reception the Religion Department hosted in honor of Father Daniel Berrigan, the peace activist. By the time I arrived, the place was crowded, alive and buzzing with conversation.

211

I milled around, greeting colleagues and engaging in light banter, when suddenly from across the room, my attention was captured by the most riveting pair of eyes I had ever seen. They were so intense they virtually burned in their sockets.

They belonged, I soon learned, to a Trappist monk who had just completed a three-year silent retreat. This evening was his first public outing.

The intensity this stranger radiated was startling. The sense of intimacy I experienced in his presence was palpable. He seemed to be giving each of us the same single-minded attention he had given all his days of prayerful solitude.

Being wholly present is a form of intimacy with life itself. Experiencing life without an overlay of expectations, projections, and judgments is a rare occurrence for most of us. To sustain this kind of attention, undistracted by hidden, self-serving agendas, requires deep humility and openness.

Real intimacy is derived from creative listening. It cannot be manufactured, nor is it the result of an applied technique. And listening with an agenda to manipulate rather than to respect another, as common a practice as this is, inevitably destroys intimacy.

The motivation behind creative listening is not to fix, change, or control those around us, but to experience and understand them on their own terms. To do so, we must let go of any need for the world to be some particular way in order to please us.

INDEPENDENCE

Are your friends safe
in the jungle of your mind?

~ Enid Ellison Cutler

Intimacy and independence go hand in hand. Dependency in an intimate relationship tends to stunt personal growth. Asking another to undertake the responsibility of being our 'other half,' an age-old description of the romantic ideal, is an impossible burden to our partner and a vain hope for us.

As we have affirmed before, real responsibility resides in the ability to respond. Responding to the *whole* of our inner and outer reality – not relegating some aspect of our selves to another – is what constitutes taking responsibility for our own *wholeness*. No one can complete us. To attempt such a thing for another would be only to inhibit our own and our partner's development.

Care for something or someone beyond ourselves is perhaps intimacy's deepest motive, but this is not to be confused with losing ourselves – our own thoughts, purpose, or destiny – for another. The turn of the century poet Rainer Maria Rilke speaks emphatically to this point:[1]

> Love is at first not anything that means merging, giving
> over, and uniting with another (for what would a union be
> of something unclarified and unfinished, still subordinate
> – ?), it is a high inducement to the individual to ripen, to
> become something in himself … for another's sake....

Chery's mother once observed that individuals often expect their marriage partners to be the answer to everything, to be the all-in-all in their lives. When this fantasy inevitably fails to materialize, she noted, they are apt to turn around in anger and to attack their spouses as the source of all their problems.

In other words, the presence of another does not ensure completeness or happiness. It is rather the mental state of oneness with life around us that engenders a sense of belonging, harmony, and joy. With the improvisational mind, anyone we encounter becomes, in some sense, an intimate.

---

1   Rainer Maria Rilke, *Ibid.*

Intimacy with Strangers

The inability to love is the central problem,
because that inability masks a certain terror,
and that terror is the terror of being touched.
And if you can't be touched, you can't be changed.
And if you can't be changed, you can't be alive.

~ James Baldwin

Why does intimacy with strangers often seem so easy? Because we assume this momentary contact will entail no lasting consequences. Nonetheless, at times, when we listen sincerely – wanting only to understand the other, without distraction, judgment, or agenda – such encounters can have real value, even provide an enduring model of intimacy at its best.

Of course, intimacy in any situation has its perils. If we listen selectively – to self and other, for instance, but not to environment – an awkward or problematic intimacy may emerge. This is the classic situation in extra-marital affairs, where two people listen only to themselves and fail to pay attention to the larger context of their lives. But awkward intimacies can happen more innocently as well.

Ran: Late one Sunday evening, I found myself picking up a few items at the local supermarket. I pushed my cart into an empty checkout lane and began to unload my basket. I had a vague sense that something about the checkout clerk was incongruous with her surroundings. In a smart, black suit, she was dressed to the nines.

The two of us began with polite chatter about the weather, and then about how it was we had each ended up late Sunday night in a supermarket. The clerk said she had taken the job a few months before, because she could not bear being alone at night after her eighteen-year-old daughter had been killed. She said holidays were the worst, but even Sundays were impossible.

I listened with rapt attention as her story spilled out. Uncertain what to say and deeply moved, I watched her as she continued to scan my groceries, tears streaming down her face.

Finally, she finished the checkout, and I paid up. By this time, I had sensed another customer lingering discreetly a few feet back. There was only one clerk in the store, so I had to move on.

The clerk and I talked a little longer, and she began to pull herself together. As she did so, I worried, "Have I done it again? Has my insufferable curiosity overrun my sensitivity to social context and caused this woman harm?" Apparently unfazed, the clerk, on the other hand, seemed appreciative of this unexpected moment and not at all embarrassed.

I wished her well and left. Driving home, I reflected on the depth of our brief exchange. The whole encounter felt like a very special improvisation, an experience of profound, if transitory, intimacy.

For many of us, intimacy with another human being is among our highest aspirations. Whether momentary or lifelong, intimacy can fill us with joy, with a sense of connection, of direction and meaning, of purpose and service beyond ourselves. It is a powerful force.

Yet intimacy can also be a fragile thing. It depends wholly upon our ability to 'keep the conversation going.' If either party becomes fearful or bored (often just another mask for fear), listening will diminish, and the relationship likely flounder.

Without exception, every intimate relationship is a 'cross-cultural' gamble. No matter what commonality exists, intimate relationships are always between two strangers, each daring to touch the mystery of the other.

Chery: In the early years of their marriage, the story goes, my parents quarreled over some issue no one remembers and ceased speaking to one another for several days. Though only a two-year-old at the time, I became their go-between.

My mother recalls feeling hopeless that they would ever find a way to reconciliation. I cannot but imagine they both did some long and deep thinking over this interlude.

On the third day of the standoff, both parents were sitting at the kitchen table eating breakfast. Apparently impressed with the importance of maintaining the silence, I went over to my father and whispered in his ear. I then walked around the table to my mother and whispered to her the same secret. End of silence.

"But what did I say?" I asked years later, when my parents recounted this story.

"I love you," they smiled in unison.

Intimacy requires a humility that leaves no strangers. We may hunger for closeness and warmth, or reaching beyond that, for core validation – to be deeply seen, understood, needed, loved. But ultimately, the acts of giving and forgiving become gifts to the giver even more than to the receiver, opportunities and inducements to deepen and grow.

As Leo Tolstoy wrote, "I believe that the meaning of life ... is only in the enlarging of love in oneself...."[2]

ROMANTICISM

The world fears a new experience
more than it fears anything.

~ D. H. Lawrence

A delusional element, however, often accompanies one form of intimacy especially – romantic relationships. All too often, we project onto our romantic partners qualities we desire them to have, refusing to acknowledge any discrepancy between our fantasy and their reality.

---

2   Leo Tolstoy, *Complete Collected Works*, volume 34, translated by Priscilla Meyer, Moscow, 1928-1958.

In such cases, whenever 'the other' behaves 'out of character,' fear takes over. The object of our affections (or is that projections?) is doing something we did not foresee. We feel out of control, and in the presence of this fear, intimacy becomes endangered.

At other times, our expectations may take the form not of a fantasy, but of a refusal to countenance change in our partner. To live fifty years with the 'same' person is impossible. More than a few transformations will occur over such a span. If we experience these changes as so fearful that we stop listening, then instead of growing with our partner, we will grow apart.

CHANGE

If we couldn't see the same objects
differently at different times,
they would die.

~ Christian W. H. Dorring

The stimulation we experience in growth is essential to life, but the changes it involves can be intimidating. In intimate relationships, we often find ourselves hovering between the excitement and the fear of change.

As disruptive as it may sometimes be, however, change *per se* does not pose a threat to intimacy. In fact, without change, intimacy will eventually die.

To assume we know another so well that we cease to listen with expectancy to what he or she will do or say, eventually renders us deaf and blind. In such cases, whether our partner physically leaves or remains, he or she gradually becomes invisible and inaudible to us and slips away.

Chery remembers her mother often speaking with delight of the husband she had listened to for fifty years, "I never know what that man will say next!"

It was evident in the animated way they conversed that both partners felt the same. The interest and attention one showed the other was a perpetual source of renewal between them.

Boundaries and Timing

There is nothing either good or bad
but thinking makes it so.

~ William Shakespeare

Two people attempting intimacy, one with boundaries 'too porous' and the other 'too rigid,' often find their efforts seriously imperiled.

For the person whose boundaries are too porous, intimacy may become overwhelming. This partner may feel overrun, unable to distinguish between his or her own thoughts and feelings, and those of the other. For the partner whose boundaries are too rigid, intimacy may seem beyond reach, leaving him or her feeling lonely and abandoned.

Similarly, the speed at which a relationship moves and changes is a delicate issue. To the degree that one party is urging the relationship forward or the other dragging his or her heels, fear may arise and undermine the ability of both to listen. When this happens, the likelihood that intimacy will survive diminishes.

Differences between individual responses to boundaries and time commonly surface in movement improvisations and can generate rich creative tension for dances. The same creativity may also be engendered by such diversity in real life relationships – or not.

If partners are willing to identify and work though the fears underlying their differences, both may find their range of thought and experience expanded and enriched. On the other hand, if their differences create a tension too great to support healthy growth, the relationship may eventually become unendurable.

SPACE

*Make the familiar strange
and the strange familiar.*

~ Bertold Brecht

Intimacy is a continuous negotiation of the space between. How close are we? How close do we dare become? And space is not just an individual preference, but a cultural one. People from some cultures seek greater emotional or physical proximity than those from other cultures.

Ran: Recently, I read about a Marine who was complaining of difficulties that many American military personnel were facing in Iraq. Most American troops, he said, did not understand that Iraqis customarily converse in each other's faces.

When challenged by a patrolling Marine, the Iraqi's natural tendency is to move in close. Even under normal circumstances, this behavior would make most Americans uncomfortable. But the possibility that the Iraqi might be carrying a bomb makes such proximity unbearable.

The negotiation of a mutually satisfying distance between people with divergent cultural backgrounds or political intentions requires profound listening. But even individuals of the same nationality will have different comfort zones, where the contact feels too close for one party or too distant for another.

The challenge is to find at what point the space negotiated between persons of differing spatial sensibility – whether emotional or physical – produces the most beneficial creative tension.

MARRIAGE

Love is a choice
not simply, or necessarily, a rational choice,
but rather a willingness to be present to others
without pretence or guile.

~ Carter Heyward

As the nucleus of the family unit, marriage has formed the foundation of social order in all societies. Technically speaking, marriage is a social institution constructed to support, strengthen, and protect the generation of humankind. Symbolically, it represents the most intimate of human associations.

But regardless of physical proximity, living arrangements, or legal bonds, the intimacy of which we are speaking is essentially mental. For this reason, what is commonly referred to as 'sexual intimacy,' even in a marriage, may not be intimate at all.

Listening without fear is the real essence of intimacy. Responding improvisationally – listening without fear to self, other, and context – is true lovemaking, whatever form it takes. Physical intimacy is only a metaphor of this communion. Close proximity may express and celebrate an emotional closeness, but it cannot create that closeness. Indeed, physical closeness may generate the very opposite of intimacy: fear.

Likewise, marriage alone does not create intimacy. In fact, the institution of marriage with its often hidden expectations and its historical assumption of hierarchy has sabotaged the intimacy of many an unsuspecting couple.

In most societies, marital hierarchy has been perpetuated on not only one, but a number of levels – physical, political, and financial. One illustration lies in the traditional notion of women as property.

Historically, marriage has often been coupled with family property arrangements, in which the wife is regarded virtually, if not literally, as part and parcel of a real estate deal. If a husband thinks of his wife in this way, chances are he will have little incentive to listen to her. Why should he? He owns her.

By contrast, if we turn to improvisation for a model of intimacy, we find a very different dynamic. In an improvisation, the dancers are separate and equal. Their relationship is a choice, negotiated moment by moment.

With the traditional model of marriage, two people are said to become 'one flesh,' meaning all too often that the wife becomes an extension of the husband. In improvisation, no one individual is ever an extension of another.

An improvisational duet is an alliance where both partners seek to be of 'one mind' – the improvisational mind – where one party does not struggle with, dominate, or capitulate to the other, but each independently follows his or her own still, small voice. Without relinquishing autonomy, both strive to yield up fear and willfulness for listening and receptivity.

To actually practice this form of 'oneness' requires the opposite of hierarchical power politics. It requires respect for self and other, and the vital trust that grows from such respect.

The word 'respect' derives from the Latin *respicere*, which means 'to look at again' or 'to look back at.' In this sense, respect means to pay attention, and then pay attention again, so that the other is seen – *really* seen. In being fully recognized, he or she feels sincerely valued, not carelessly taken for granted.

In his widely read bestseller, Malcolm Gladwell cites the work of John Gottman, when addressing the question of respect and hierarchy in marriage:[3]

---

3   Malcolm Gladwell, *Blink: The Power of Thinking Without Thinking*, New York: Little, Brown and Company, 2005.

If Gottman observes one or both partners in a marriage showing contempt toward the other, he considers it the single most important sign that the marriage is in trouble.

Contempt derives from a sense of superiority and disdain. And this never leads to listening or intimacy. The appearance of contempt is a sure sign that respect and trust, two critical elements of both marriage and improvisation, have broken down.

From his research into the longevity of marriage relationships, Gottman identifies four forms of interaction that signal trouble: criticism, defensiveness, stonewalling, and contempt.

The first two and even the third indicate some form of interaction between equals. But with contempt, a disconnection takes place, as the assumption of equality is replaced by that of superiority/inferiority.

As Ran found, first in *Sonomama* and then in his counseling work with couples, where a struggle between equals exists, no matter how heated, there is hope. But when either or both partners cease to listen, it can mean only one of two things: the dance is in serious trouble, or it is over.

In its best sense, the institution of marriage, like a good improvisational structure, provides boundaries meant to stimulate, protect, and support the creativity and growth of each party. It affords two people a partnership within which to work out their individual lives, to deepen their foundations and expand their horizons.

Within the boundaries of this relationship, both parties find concurrently the freedom to be themselves and the imperative to move beyond themselves – for their own sakes, and for the sake of the other.

INFIDELITY

I believe that every single event in life
happens as an opportunity
to choose love over fear.

~ Oprah Winfrey

Ideally in an intimate relationship, we want to remain open to and supportive of the growth and development of the other individual. But in practice, this often proves a challenge.

The desire to manipulate another is a temptation that at times can seem almost irresistible. Refraining from acting on this desire requires that we ourselves not be manipulated by fear.

To be intimate with another is to accept that in some essential way we are not in the driver's seat of our own destiny, that we do not have command over a major investment in our lives. No sovereign control, no master plan. Intimacy is a genuine improvisation.

Nowhere is this more apparent than when a marital partner, seeking outer stimulation, embarks upon an affair. Expectations based upon the marriage vows are shattered. If the marriage is to continue, both members must face the demand to uncover and overcome their fears and replace those fears with listening.

Many times a marriage will not survive this rupture of trust. However, to move forward constructively into whatever the future holds, both partners owe it to themselves and all concerned to do the deep listening to self and other that affords the only path to resolution.

If intimacy is to endure over the long term, the partners in any relationship need to be skilled improvisers. They must commit themselves each day to a new improvisation. Intimacy takes nothing for granted. It greets every day with an improvisational mind.

RENEWAL

The real thing
is to be saturated with something –
that is, in one way or another,
with life.

~ William James

Listening connotes interest and respect, and these mental qualities provide the underpinnings for communication. Even in the face of continual shifts in a marriage or sudden, unexpected life changes, interest and respect, like two steel spans of a bridge, make a way for love to pass over.

But what if these two elements should diminish or, at some point in a relationship, disappear altogether? Is there any recourse?

Fortunately, both interest and respect can be nurtured and regained, and naturally, we feel the best way to do so is through listening. Our work with improvisation is filled with analogies of this process of renewal.

In the midst of an improvisation, we sometimes find ourselves unexpectedly at a dead end. The movement we have been pursuing suddenly dries up. Everything we try seems devoid of interest or energy. We feel stymied, exposed, bereft, lost.

In our chapter on *Idleness*, we spoke of these episodes in our lives as the 'empty' spaces or the 'wild' spaces of transitional experience. In our chapter, *The Improvisational Mind*, we described the same phenomenon as our entering a state of liminality.

In the specific context of a long-term intimate relationship, the identical need for renewal arises. Relationships, like any living thing, require periods of regeneration.

In our *Creative Listening* workshops, we offer dancers three movement options to consider when interest wanes and inspiration fails: *repeat, borrow*, or *be still*. Of course, all three alternatives are only aids in fostering the real source of creative renewal – a recommitted and intensified return to listening.

> **Repeat** – The first option is not to change anything at all, but simply to focus more deeply on whatever we are presently doing. Instead of casting our current activity aside as unsatisfying, we can do the reverse. We can repeat it and repeat it and repeat it with intensified awareness and commitment, no matter how poor or insignificant the activity may initially appear. Bringing all our concentration to this moment of limbo is like blowing on a hot coal. With persistence and patience, we begin to kindle the creative possibilities hidden in seemingly lifeless circumstances, and the fire of creativity reignites.

> **Borrow** – The second option is to open our attention to the ideas and activities of others around us. If we catch the wave of their energy, we can follow along in their wake for a while, until our own creative energies begin to flow again.

> **Be Still** – The third option may be the most challenging. Remaining alert in a state of stillness – not pushing forward into motion prematurely nor sinking into passivity and mindlessness – requires a discipline and trust developed only with practice. But deepest of the three, this option is especially effective at defining moments in a dance or in life.

Obviously, all three options have real life applications, especially in times of relational transition. 'Repeat' suggests redoubling our efforts to more closely and earnestly attend the work we are doing or the relationship we are in. 'Borrow' suggests seeking outside ourselves for rejuvenation, as in taking a vacation or workshop, attending a lecture or concert, or turning to a counselor for perspective and guidance. 'Be still' suggests turning to meditation or prayer, going on retreat, or simply taking a walk.

SELECTIVE LISTENING

If you are afraid of loneliness,
don't marry.

~ Anton Chekhov

In our workshops, we have an improvisational structure called 'Agenda Dances,' where dancers are assigned fixed agendas. As usual, dancers are expected to listen, but because they are also following an agenda, their listening will be at best selective.

The agendas are designed to produce interesting dances, yet they have obvious parallels to life practice as well. Agendas include:

Self-only – Attention is focused almost exclusively on self-generated impulses to act.

Other-only – Attention is focused almost exclusively on impulses to act generated by others.

Theme-only – Attention is focused almost exclusively on pursuing a single theme or line of action.

Caprice-only – Attention flits, theme-less, from one disconnected impulse to another.

By our definition, a performative state of mind and an intimate state of mind are one and the same – the state of paying attention without fear. This may explain in some measure why the theater-going public paradoxically feels a sense of intimacy with performers they have never personally met.

Given the coincidence of performing and intimacy, what happens in the performance of an 'Agenda Duet,' where the listening of one of the dancers is compromised?

If only one performer is listening, a good improvisation – a state of intimacy with the audience, at least – may still transpire. But given their inequality of attention, will a state of intimacy *between the two performers* occur?

The listening dancer may experience the intimacy of being alive to self, partner, and environment, and the audience will share in that intimacy. The selective listener will probably fail to feel the intimacy at the time of the performance. In reflecting back on the situation, however, this dancer may experience retrospectively the intimacy offered by his or her partner.

The same holds true in relationships. At times, one partner may be distracted by an agenda and not fully available. But this need not prevent the other from continuing with the 'improvisation.' And on looking back, the selective listener may appreciate deeply the support his or her partner provided during that interval through patient and persistent attention.

In the case of long-term relationships, intimacy seems to ebb and flow. Sometimes our own or our partner's interest is high, and at other times listening becomes selective or altogether drops away. But we *can* live an intimate life, even during periods when our partner is not listening.

This frees us from one of the fears of committed relationships: that we are dependent on another's listening for intimacy. We do not have to control our partner to experience a state of intimacy. We have only to control our own thought and action.

Chery & Ran: In a workshop where we introduced 'Agenda Dances,' [Luke] and [Callie] performed an 'Agenda Duet.' Luke was assigned the role of 'creative listener.' The role of 'selective listener' fell to Callie, who decided to assume the 'self-only' agenda.

We learned later that Callie had chosen this agenda because it was opposite to 'other-only,' the role she tended to take in day-to-day life, while she described her boyfriend (who was not present at this workshop) as commonly exhibiting 'self-only' listening tendencies.

For several years, the two had struggled with these differences. Now, through an 'Agenda Duet,' Callie saw an opportunity both to explore her boyfriend's habitual role and to observe how another person, cast in her customary role, would handle their relational dynamic.

Given the intensity of Callie's commitment to her 'self-only' agenda, Luke had his work cut out for him. He tried everything under the sun to get something going between the two of them, but Callie was steadfast. She remained staunchly insular.

Finally, in frustration, Luke grasped Callie's feet and spun her around him in a circle on the floor. He seemed reduced, the audience later remarked, to a proverbial caveman.

Callie was delighted. Just to have someone acknowledge how challenging her real-life role was, provided a sense of confirmation and support. But beyond that, she was curious to identify and discuss what options existed for her in this relationship.

The audience pointed out that, in his attempt to elicit some kind of interaction, Luke had abandoned the one power he had to realize a successful improvisation – that of listening to himself.

Had he remembered that option, Luke could have continued to listen to Callie without anger or resentment, even though she refused to acknowledge him. By staying in touch with himself and his environment, chances are he would have created a compelling improvisation.

Thus engaged, he could have afforded to wait for Callie to come around. Something, of course, she still might not have done. But in any case, his time would not have been wasted.

Reflecting on this experience, Callie realized that her challenges were threefold: to accept her boyfriend as he was; to resist imposing agendas of her own on their relationship; and most important of all, not to lose herself.

In life as well as in movement improvisation, whenever we try to force someone else to change, we are setting ourselves up for disappointment. All we can do is one hundred percent of our fifty percent of a relationship. Only the frog himself, and no one else, can turn him into a prince. The transformative kiss is the stuff of fairytales.

There may come a point when we have to admit that a relationship we hoped to sustain is no longer worth the effort. At times like these, we may have to face the fact that we have learned what we can and need to move on.

MOTIVE

For finally, we are as we love.
It is love that measures
our stature.

~ William Sloane Coffin

Intimacy cannot be engineered, because it eludes any kind of control one individual may wield over another. For true intimacy, motive is all-important. And as we have said before, that motive must never be to possess, change, or profit from the other, but rather to experience and understand the other 'just as he or she is.'

This is not to say that such respect and love is without effect. Seen and cherished for themselves, people often do change. They change their *own* lives – and flourish.

Developing the safety required for intimacy demands honesty from both parties in a relationship, honesty first with oneself, and then with the other. The following story of prison conversations with a convicted criminal may seem an incongruous illustration in a chapter on intimacy, but it elucidates

with especial clarity an important point about the foundation of relationships and community.

*Chery: Steve spent many years as a prosecutor before becoming a federal appellate
circuit court judge. He has seen more of the world's ills, I believe, than anyone else
I know.*

*One day, in answer to a question of mine, he declared, "I can tell you in one word
the heart of crime: selfishness. Any step towards overcoming selfishness is a step
towards eradicating crime."*

*He then related the story of Stanley, a man he had prosecuted for a series of horrific
felonies. What my friend found unnerving about this man was not the nature of
his crimes (sadly, Steve had seen that kind of thing many times before), but how
thoroughly normal Stanley appeared.*

*Stanley was an engaging, affable man, a good conversationalist. To the world, he
seemed just a 'nice guy.' And it was this appearance of normality that had been his
best disguise, enabling him to elude arrest for years.*

*Steve was intrigued. Over his career, he had finely honed his ability to read char-
acter, but here was a man who had deceived so many. Steve wondered if somehow
he could learn to detect the mentality that lay behind Stanley's appalling crimes.*

*Following Stanley's life sentence, Steve visited him in the penitentiary from time
to time for lunch and conversation. After a number of these visits, my friend told
me, he "finally got it."*

*"What did you see?" I wanted to know. "Was it his eyes, his voice, some kind of
disconnect?"*

*None of the above. What Steve detected was "a duality of thought." He saw that
where Stanley was concerned, there were perpetually two things going on: what
he appeared to be saying or doing and what he was really after.*

Stanley always had an angle. Right and wrong meant nothing to him; he was totally devoid of conscience. The hidden motive that lay behind everything he did was rank, short-term self-interest.

Steve was eventually able to decode Stanley's intent in any act or statement simply by asking himself, "What's in it for Stanley?"

Of course, not every selfish act is deemed by our judicial system a crime. But in the larger sense, that is exactly what it is – if not a crime against another, then surely a crime against ourselves. It ultimately robs us of our most precious possessions: empathy and love. And it bars us from what most people consider the dearest comforts of human experience – inner peace, a sense of worth, and true friendship.

SELF-LOVE VS. SELFISHNESS

Finally, brethren, whatsoever things are true,
whatsoever things are honest,
whatsoever things are just,
whatsoever things are pure,
whatsoever things are lovely,
whatsoever things are of good report,
... think on these things.

~ Saint Paul

What is selfishness and how does it differ from healthy self-love? *Webster's Comprehensive Dictionary* is explicit upon this point:

> *Self-love* is due care for one's own happiness and well-being, which is perfectly compatible with justice, generosity, or benevolence toward others; *selfishness* is an undue or exclusive care for one's own comfort or pleasure, regardless of the happiness, and often of the rights, of others. *Self-love* is necessary to high endeavor, and even to self-

preservation; *selfishness* limits endeavor to a narrow circle
of intensely personal aims.

How do we overcome selfishness? We begin by stripping off its cover and exposing its root: fear. Every expression of selfishness, as distinguished from healthy self-love, is an expression of insecurity. Regardless of how swaggering or supercilious the perpetrator, insecurity and fear underlie every selfish act.

But selfishness inevitably boomerangs. The greatest torment of the dishonest man, the saying goes, is not that he will be found out, but that he can trust no one else to be truthful. Thus, he allows the fear behind his dishonesty to rob him of his basis for intimacy – trust, respect, and empathy.

The selfishness that impels us to prey upon others ultimately removes us in one way or another from the privilege of society and community. Intimacy, the deepest expression of community, requires the solid ground of trust and respect, and cannot take root in selfishness or fear.

Handling and overcoming fear is no small task. But we believe this undertaking has its beginnings in our attention, and where and how we place that attention. Our own safety in a relationship begins when we move from asking what we can get, to asking what we can give, "What does the dance need?"

INTIMATE PRESENCE

Never believe that a few caring people
can't change the world.
For, indeed, that's all who ever have.

~ Margaret Mead

When it comes to intimacy, we must begin with ourselves. No matter who or what or how the *other* person in a relationship is, intimacy is not possible for us if *we* are not there.

Chery: There is the allegorical story of a candle, sent into the world to seek out all the places of darkness on the earth. The candle travels far and wide, searching every cave and cavern, penetrating every hidden space, to the farthest boundaries of the earth.

Finally, after countless days and nights of journeying, the candle returns despondent and defeated. Its mission has been a failure. Try as it might, it could find no place of darkness anywhere.

Intimacy begins not with the presence of certain, specific people or circumstances in our lives, but with our own presence of mind. It begins with paying attention without fear to that still, small, inner voice.

Once the foundation of inner listening is established, our attention may safely expand to embrace others, indeed the world, in the intimacy of improvisation. And listening without fear for ourselves, we will find intimacy everywhere.

COMMENCEMENT

On with the dance!
let joy be unconfined ...

~ Lord Byron

Of course, this is not the conclusion to our journey; it is only another begin-ning. A life on the creative edge is a challenging, ever-engaging, ongoing process.

The practice of creative listening is much like a seed. Beginning with a single dance, it may continue to propagate over the seasons of a lifetime. The critical factor is the soil into which the seed falls – our receptivity of thought.

It has been our contention throughout this book that creativity is not a tal-ent reserved for the gifted few; it is a discipline that can be learned. Unlike most disciplines, creative listening is applicable to virtually any situation and endeavor, and is as vital to cultivating community as it is to nurturing creativity.

In our *Creative Listening* workshops, as in our lives, we have repeatedly witnessed how the success or failure of human interactions is determined not so much by the presence or absence of differences, as by the presence or absence of listening.

How often do we take a moment to step back, especially in the midst of disagreement, and pay attention with true appreciation to another 'just as they are?' But what a gift we give and receive in this one small act.

Developing tolerance, compassion, and respect for another, let alone humankind with all its diversity, is an aspiration easily voiced, but difficult to sustain. At base, it involves confronting ourselves and overcoming fear through the transformative power of listening.

But so much for theory and talk. Sooner or later, we each face the moment when we are called not just to profess, but to practice what we believe – in short, to 'shut up and dance.'

Index of Authors Cited

About the Authors

CHERYL VARIAN CUTLER – B.A. Sarah Lawrence College; M.A. Wesleyan University; C.M.A. University of Washington. Co-founder of *Listening Unlimited*. Dance Department founder, former dance professor and chair at Wesleyan University for thirty-two years. Co-founder of *Sonomama Improvisation Dance Theater*. Recipient of the *First Annual Wesleyan University Award for Teaching Excellence*.

RANDALL HUNTSBERRY – B.A., Ph.D. Harvard University. Co-founder of *Listening Unlimited*. Poet. Corporate consultant/leadership coach. Former marriage and family counselor. Former professor of comparative religions at Wesleyan University. Co-founder of *Sonomama Improvisation Dance Theater*. Author of *Listening Out Loud: The Leadership Paradox*.

Information on workshops and publications by the authors is available at www.ListeningUnlimited.com

About the Cover

Photo by ROBERT JOHN BLAKERS – B.S. (Hons) Australian National University. Environmental activist. Photographer. Publisher of *Wilderness Tasmania* calendars and diaries for sixteen years. Publisher of photographic books *Cradle* and *Freycinet*.

Information on photography and publications by Robert Blakers is available at www.robblakers.com